Reaching God Through Conversation

Dorothy M. Johnson
Mary J. Lee
Eric S. Lee
with comments by Willie Johnson

J AN L PRODUCTIONS LLC

Unless otherwise noted, all scripture is
from the *King James Version* of the Bible.

Scripture quotations taken from *The Amplified Bible* (AMP),
Copyright © 1954, 1958, 1962, 1964, 1965, 1987 by
The Lockman Foundation. All rights reserved.
Used by permission. (www.Lockman.org)

Scripture quotations taken from the *Complete Jewish Bible* (CJB),
Copyright © 1998 by David H. Stern. All rights reserved.

Scripture quotations taken from *The Living Bible* (TLB),
Copyright © 1971 by Tyndale House Foundation.
Used by permission of Tyndale House Publishers Inc.,
Carol Stream, Illinois 60158. All rights reserved.

Scripture quotations taken from *The Expanded Bible* (EXB),
Copyright © 2011 by Thomas Nelson Inc. All rights reserved.

Scripture taken from the *Good News Translation - Second Edition* (GNT),
Copyright by American Bible Society. Used by permission.
(The Good News Translation -The Holy Bible Online)

Scripture taken from *The New King James Bible, New Testament* (NKJV),
Copyright © 1979, 1982, 1994 by Thomas Nelson, Inc.
The New King James Bible, New Testament & Psalms, Copyright © 1980
by Thomas Nelson, Inc. Used by permission. All rights reserved

Scripture taken from The Holy Bible, *New International Version*® (NIV),
Copyright © 1973, 1978, 1984, 2011 by Biblica, Inc.®
Used by permission. All rights reserved worldwide.

Scripture quotations taken from the *English Standard Version* (ESV).
The Holy Bible, English Standard Version, Copyright © 2001 by
Crossway Bibles, a publishing ministry of Good News Publishers.

Printed in the United States of America.

ACKNOWLEDGMENT

We would like to express our thanks first and foremost to our Lord and Savior Jesus Christ and in retrospect to our brother and brother-in-law Willie for seeing in some of us what we did not see in ourselves — a book. Rick, Mary's husband and our brother-in-law is already an author. We are also appreciative of others (family, friends and spiritual mentors) who encouraged us along the way. Willie had been nudging us for some time to write a prayer book with the new believer in mind. We wish we could say these writings were without a hitch, but that was far from the truth. We encountered several snares along the way — from getting started, to thinking of something to say that would benefit the reader, to computer problems, distractions by others and ourselves, and countless other interruptions.

Although we live miles apart, our brother/brother-in-law Willie's words were constantly ringing in our ears, "have you gotten started yet or where are you on completing the assignment?" Finally, as our progress went from slow to stop, he said, "pray and ask God for a completion date," which we did and the Lord spoke a date through Rick. Without the Lord giving us a date, I don't know what our testimony would be for the book at this point.

We give special thanks to Eric Lee, son of Rick and Mary for his creativity in graphic design at the beginning of each chapter. Our heartfelt appreciation to Ruth Rogers for her willingness and the countless hours she spent proof reading the manuscript in the rough stages. The originality in designing a cover that speaks to the content of this book goes to Rick Lee. He is also credited for the photography. Finally, every book must have a name and the title of this book is credited to the insightful wisdom of Bishop Hubert Banks.

We pray that you will be blessed by this writing and it will help you along the way as you pray for yourself and others and become the pray-er, warrior/intercessor that God is calling you to be. Remember, God is waiting to have a conversation with you.

TABLE OF CONTENTS

Foreword xix

CHAPTER ONE
Prayer - A Vital Part of Christian Duty.............................25

CHAPTER TWO
The Believers Role in Prayer...39

CHAPTER THREE
How to Pray Individually or Corporately........................59

CHAPTER FOUR
Preparation for Prayer & Intercession 71

CHAPTER FIVE
Making the Transition from Prayer to Intercession............83

CHAPTER SIX
Developing Focus & Consistency in Prayer....................95

CHAPTER SEVEN
Discerning the Longevity of the Prayer Group 109

CHAPTER EIGHT
Handling Distractions..121

CHAPTER NINE
Trials & Tribulations..129

CHAPTER TEN
Keys to Remember..137

CHAPTER ELEVEN
Overcoming the Urge to Quit..143

CHAPTER TWELVE
Achieving Victory..151

Epilogue 157

Glossary...163

End Notes...167

Throughout this writing some personal experiences and conversations with the Lord will be shared by each of us.

FOREWORD

"Trust in the LORD with all your heart, And lean not on your own understanding." (Proverbs 3:5 - NKJV)

Many people are wondering how to reach God through conversation; however we must first acknowledge His Word according to Proverbs 3:6, "In all your ways acknowledge Him, And He shall direct your paths" (NKJV). As we go through life's journey, there ought to be daily communication with God. He is expecting us to have daily conversation with Him and one of the greatest things we should do is listen for a response for we are admonished in His Word that's recorded in John 15:7, "If you abide in Me, and My words abide in you, you will ask what you desire, and it shall be done for you" (NKJV).

It is important to understand that our Heavenly Father desires that we be blessed in every aspect of our lives. He even sent His only begotten Son Jesus Christ that we might have life and that more abundantly. The Gospel of John: 10:10 tells us that, "The thief does not come except to steal, and to kill, and to destroy. I have come that they may have life, and that they may have it more abundantly" (NKJV). As you read this book, it is my sincere prayer that you will be blessed above and beyond your greatest expectation and that you will see the manifestation of your prayers being answered. Many people are praying but not reaching God. I am confident that the depth of real life experiences shared in this book will greatly impact your life as it did mine through everyday conversations with God.

Prayer is also offered for those who have labored in the writing of this book as a family, which exemplifies the importance of families praying together, and that they would be the recipients of a great harvest of seeing families start coming together in prayer throughout the world in greater numbers.

I am reminded of the words of the Hymnal "Have a little talk with Jesus…" by Cleavant Derricks. God is waiting to hear what is on your heart.

Bishop Hubert Banks
Founder/Pastor, PDT *(Pentecostal Deliverance Tabernacle)* Worship Center
& PDOM *(Pentecostal Deliverance Outreach Ministries)*
Westwood, New Jersey

RIDDLE

Scripture: Judges 14:14

Out of the eater came forth meat,
and out of the strong came forth sweetness

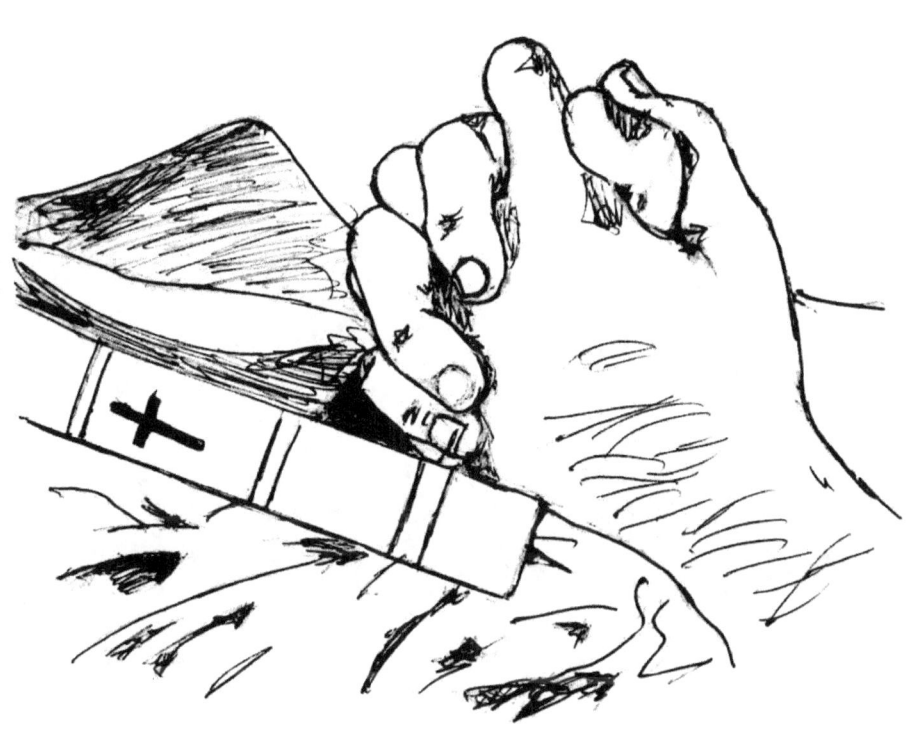

CHAPTER ONE

Prayer - A Vital Part of Christian Duty

The definition of prayer as defined by Webster Dictionary: a petition, supplication, entreaty; that which is asked; however, plain and simple — prayer is having a conversation with God. You talk to God, then you listen and He talks back to you. The Word admonishes believers in 1 Thessalonians 5:17 to "pray without ceasing," which does not mean that we should be on our knees all the time, rather that we should stay in an attitude of prayer. We should always be conscious of the Presence of God and that He is available to talk to us at anytime. God wants us to "draw near to Him," as stated in (James 4:8a NKJV) in fellowship and worship. It is a humbling thought to know that God, the Creator of the Universe wants to fellowship with you and me. God is interested in hearing what we have to say and as a good Father, He wants to bless us through answered prayer. God delights in giving us the desires of our heart — as long as what is desired is in alignment with His Word. God wants us to trust Him with our life because He truly knows what's best for us. The prophet Jeremiah declared, "Before I formed you in the womb I knew you…" (Jeremiah 1:5a NKJV).

Prayer is a link to God. It is a form of communication that represents a relationship. Most often, in times past we learn it in innocence and simplicity such as bedtime prayer and hone it in repetition and spiritual growth. It does not require pomp and circumstance. Jesus said to the disciples, "And when you pray, you shall not be like the hypocrites. For they love to pray standing in the synagogues and on the corners of the streets, that they may be seen by men. Assuredly, I say to you, they have their reward. But you, when you pray, go into your room, and when you have shut the door, pray to your Father who is in the secret place; and your Father who sees in secret will reward you openly" (Matthew 6:5-6 NKJV).

The questions, concerns, needs and situations in your life may seem overwhelming and insurmountable. Take comfort in knowing that this is not the case! The devil is a liar who only comes to confuse us so that he may destroy us. But our God sent hope through Jesus our Savior as is stated in

John's Gospel, "The thief does not come, except to steal, and to kill, and to destroy. I have come that they may have life, and that they may have it more abundantly" (John 10:10 NKJV). Don't get confused wondering if you should pray about the things of concern in your life. God makes it clear in His Word that we are not only to pray, under the direction of the Holy Spirit, but we are to expect answers, and we will receive them.

Luke 11:5-10

5   "And he said unto them, Which of you shall have a friend, and shall go unto him at midnight, and say unto him, Friend, lend me three loaves;

6   For a friend of mine in his journey is come to me, and I have nothing to set before him?"

7   And he from within shall answer and say, Trouble me not: the door is now shut, and my children are with me in bed; I cannot rise and give thee.

8   I say unto you, Though he will not rise and give him, because he is his friend, yet because of his importunity he will rise and give him as many as he needeth.

9   And I say unto you, Ask, and it shall be given you; seek, and ye shall find; knock, and it shall be opened unto you.

10 For every one that asketh receiveth; and he that seeketh findeth; and to him that knocketh; it shall be opened."

Luke 18:1

"And he spake a parable unto them to this end, that men ought always to pray, and not to faint;"

1 Timothy 2:8

"I will therefore that men pray every where, lifting up holy hands, without wrath and doubting."

Psalm 134:2

"Lift up your hands in the sanctuary, and bless the LORD."

Hebrews 4:14, 16

14 Seeing then that we have a great high priest, that is passed into the heavens, Jesus the Son of God, let us hold fast our profession.

16 Let us therefore come boldly unto the throne of grace, that we may obtain mercy, and find grace to help in time of need."

Prayer is an important tool — rather it's a must have device that Christians can't live without. It is necessary because it allows us as believers to become strong in our Christian walk and build a relationship with our Heavenly Father. God wants to be intimately involved in our lives. A conversation engages at least two people.

And as it relates to prayer, it's between you and God. His talking to us is done in various ways such as: when we read the Bible, pray, the preached Word, talk to other believers or just sit quietly and listen for God to speak (through a prompting or a strong sense of knowing[1]) into our spirit what He wants to tell us. There will be times when we will question whether or not what we are hearing is God speaking or is Satan speaking. Jesus said in John 10:27, "My sheep hear my voice, and I know them, and they follow me:" One way to test whether or not it is the Lord speaking to you is to ask God for a Scripture to support what has been heard.[2]

KEEPING IT SIMPLE

Simple is good. You can start where you are and at your level of faith. You may not have the faith of someone you may see as a so-called "**spiritual giant**," because as a new believer you may not have developed your faith. As you mature in the things of God you will have to grow your faith on purpose. But rest assured God meets us at our point of need and at our level of belief. The Bible says in Romans 12:3, "For I say, through the grace given unto me, to every man that is among you, not to think of himself more highly than he ought to think; but to think soberly, according as God hath dealt to every man the measure of faith."

The Word tells us that Jesus' finished work on the Cross of Calvary made it possible for the believer to go from faith to faith and glory to glory, as declared in Romans 1:17, "For therein is the righteousness of God revealed from faith to faith: as it is written, The just shall live by faith." And II Corinthians 3:18 states, "But we all, with open face beholding as in a glass the glory of the Lord, are changed into the same image from glory to glory, even as by the Spirit of the Lord." Hence in light of God's Word, that "spiritual giant" probably feels that he or she is still not where they need to be. That just means we should always be moving and growing in our faith. I Peter 2:2 states, "As newborn babes, desire the sincere milk of the word, that ye may grow thereby:" As we grow we begin to get increased revelation of the different **facets** and levels of God. Who He is and what He will do: His trustworthiness, His faithfulness, His unending mercy and grace, His peace and His promises are just some of the things revealed to and in us. Jesus declared in John 14:27, "Peace I leave with you, my peace I give unto you: not as the world giveth…" So, use the faith you have no matter how much or how little you think it is. Ask the Lord to help your unbelief because He is more than able and more than willing to help you at anytime whenever there is a need. Draw from the encouragement in these Scriptures:

Mark 9:14-27

14 And when he came to his disciples, he saw a great multitude about them, and the scribes questioning with them.

15 And straightway all the people, when they beheld him, were greatly amazed, and running to him saluted him.

16 And he asked the scribes, What question ye with them?

17 And one of the multitude answered and said, Master, I have brought unto thee my son, which hath a dumb spirit;

18 And wheresoever he taketh him, he teareth him: and he foameth, and gnasheth with his teeth, and pineth away: and I spake to thy disciples that they should cast him out; and they could not.

19 He answereth him, and saith, O faithless generation, how long shall I be with you? How long shall I suffer you? bring him unto me.

20 And they brought him unto him: and when he saw him, straightway the spirit tare him; and he fell on the ground, and wallowed foaming.

21 And he asked his father, How long is it ago since this came unto him? And he said, Of a child.

22 And ofttimes it hath cast him into the fire, and into the waters, to destroy him: but if thou canst do any thing, have compassion on us, and help us.

23 Jesus said unto him, If thou canst believe, all things are possible to him that believeth.

24 And straightway the father of the child cried out, and said with tears, Lord, I believe; help thou mine unbelief.

25 When Jesus saw that the people came running together, he rebuked the foul spirit, saying unto him, Thou dumb and deaf spirit, I charge thee, come out of him, and enter no more into him.

26 And the spirit cried, and rent him sore, and came out of him: and he was as one dead; insomuch that many said, He is dead.

27 But Jesus took him by the hand, and lifted him up; and he arose.

NATURALLY SPEAKING

Talking with family, friends, peers, co-workers, pastors, church members and beyond is without preparation. We don't have to Google, use iPads, Tablets, Droids or iPhones before we begin a conversation — it's what we do on impulse. At the beginning stages our vocabulary may be limited on a particular subject. However as we interact on a day-to-day basis, we acquire and store up more words, phrases and ideas into our word bank for use at a later time and in different settings, such as: when we pray for children, youth, adults and professionals, etc., knowing that God will hear our prayer. David admonished in Psalm 54:2, "Hear my prayer, O God; give ear to the words of my mouth."

PAINFULLY SPEAKING

There are times when we have a discussion with God because we are hurting, frustrated and even angry. Its okay to go there, but do not stay there — it can be devastating! Those roller coaster feelings of pain are born out of emotional and physical stresses that we encounter from day to day as a result of what we do to ourselves and what we allow others to do to us. How do you talk to God out of this place that many times cannot be verbalized because it is beyond words? Sometimes we ourselves do not have a clue how we ended up at this place in our heart. However, because God knows our thoughts before they enter our subconscious, you can tell Him to the best of your ability what is disturbing your peace of mind. In Psalm 139:1 David expressed it this way, "O LORD, thou hast searched me, and known me." As a matter of fact, you can just come right out and say, "God I am mad at my sister, my brother, my friend, my pastor — and yes, God I am mad at you also." Ask Him to help you to want to renew your mind to think like He thinks so you won't get stuck in a spiritual ditch spinning your wheels trying to get out by yourself, which is a fruitless undertaking. Romans 12:2 declares, "And be not conformed to this world: but be ye transformed by the renewing of your mind, that ye may prove what is that good, and acceptable, and perfect, will of God."

SPIRITUALLY SPEAKING

New believers and even some mature believers may find it uncomfortable to pray openly or in public initially. However, spiritual growth is achieved by spending time studying the Word not just reading the Word. Practice speaking the Word to yourself in the mirror or imagine you are talking to an audience of believers, and then you will gradually begin to feel a level of comfort over time when prayer is offered outside of your private sphere of influence. The Holy Spirit will progress you into having an open conversation with God step by step while including others with special needs in your prayers. Paul encouraged the church at Ephesus when he said, "The eyes of your understanding being enlightened; that ye may know what is the hope of his calling, and what the riches of the glory of his inheritance in the saints," (Ephesians 1:18). If you are unsure of what to pray, you can ask God or look in the Scripture and pray the Word in the Name of Jesus. Jesus said, "And whatsoever ye shall ask in my name, that will I do, that the Father may be glorified in the Son" (John 14:13). Now that you have cleared out all the cobwebs and everything is in its proper place in your spiritual closet — as much as is possible at this juncture, it's time to move forward with poise and stride.

GETTING STARTED

Incorporating prayer into an already crowded schedule is sometimes difficult until the believer comes to the realization that prioritizing one's 'to do list' must always begin with the Word, prayer and time spent in God's Presence. Make up your mind and settle it in your spirit that each day must begin and end with God. David said, "O GOD, thou art my God; early will I seek thee: my soul thirsteth for thee, my flesh longeth for thee in a dry and thirsty land, where no water is;" (Psalm 63:1). God is ready and willing to give direction — if you ask Him. The Bible declares in Proverbs 3:5, "Trust in the LORD with all thine heart; and lean not unto thine own understanding." If you begin your day with God, all the other things that are demanding your attention will amazingly get done. God redeems the time by helping us set priorities. Talking to God is a perfect opportunity to tell Him how grateful you are for His blessings and to spill the innermost secrets of your heart that you are unable to share with anyone else. Ask for forgiveness of sins that you may have committed by an action or thought. Sometimes you may find it hard to share some secrets with God. You can take comfort in knowing your Heavenly Father has your best interest at heart. The Bible declares in Hebrews 4:13, "Neither is there any creature that is not manifest in his sight: but all things are naked and opened unto the eyes of him with whom we have to do." God wants the believer to talk to Him like a Father because He loves you. When praying to God, call Him "Father or Daddy." When you are talking to your natural father, you do not refer to him as Mr. Smith or Mr. French. You say daddy, father, papa, etc. You make your conversation personal, intimate, warm and kind. Jesus is our example. When He prayed, He said, "Father." The Gospel of John 11: 41, 42 records Jesus' saying, "Then they took away the stone from the place where the dead was laid. And Jesus lifted up his eyes, and said, Father, I thank thee that thou hast heard me. And I knew that thou hearest me always: but because of the people which stand by I said it, that they may believe that thou hast sent me." Pattern your conversations with God after Jesus.

THE RIGHT TIME

Choosing the right time is of utmost importance because God expects us to keep our appointment with Him. Jesus said, "…Come ye yourselves, apart into a desert place, and rest a while…" (Mark 6:31a). If it is not possible to be committed to a definite hour of prayer, consider alternatives. It is better to meet with God in the morning, at noon or in the evening at an hour that is not time specific. For example, don't **obligate** yourself to a definite time of 5:00 a.m., 7:00 a.m., 3:00 p.m., 6:00 p.m., etc., if there is any inkling you may not be able to adhere to the commitment. Meeting with God should be more exciting and important than a job interview, arriving on time to catch a flight or some other exhilarating event. Just as we give preparation to looking our best before we greet the public, we should likewise give special attention to our appearance when we meet with our Heavenly Father. In addition to being properly groomed, we are to prepare our hearts as well. Turn the searchlight inward. Ask yourself, have I spoken crossly to anyone, thought negatively about someone or am I in the right frame of mind for prayer at this time? The Psalmist David declared, "The sacrifices of God are a broken spirit: a broken and a contrite heart, O God, thou wilt not despise" (Psalm 51:17). **Conversely** meeting with the King of kings should electrify us to want to come looking better than we would if we were going to meet with an earthly person of royalty. Anticipation of this appointed time with God should spur us in our spirit to escalate with unexplainable strength. The Bible admonishes, "But grow in spiritual strength and become better acquainted with our Lord and Savior Jesus Christ…" II Peter 3:18a TLB). On the other hand, you can always rest assured that even if you have not given yourself to preparation, God will never turn you away because of His great love. Jesus said, "All that the Father giveth me shall come to me; and him that cometh to me I will in no wise cast out" (John 6:37).

A QUIET PLACE

Find a place in your mental thinking, your emotions and in your spirit to have fellowship with God. Consider your time with your Father as if you were meeting with that special someone for the very first time. When you are with that special person, you do not want any distractions. All of your time and attention is devoted to communicating with and listening to what your special friend has to say to you. Create an atmosphere that would be conducive for God to come and inhabit. David assures us that, "He WHO dwells in the secret place of the Most High shall remain stable and fixed under the shadow of the Almighty [Whose power no foe can withstand]" (Psalm 91:1 AMP). God loves the special time that you set aside to meet with Him alone. The very thought that God, the Creator of this vast universe longs to fellowship with you and me whom He created in His Image is awe-inspiring. "So God created man in his own image, in the image of God created he him; male and female created he them" (Genesis 1:27).

KEEPING IT REAL

Talking to God does not require us to get out the dictionary or the thesaurus. We can be down to earth — like talking to a friend. Perfect English is not a requirement. Just express yourself, be who you are and relax in God's

Presence with reverential comfort. "And Enoch walked with God..." (Genesis 5:22a). Our Heavenly Father can read our thoughts and the unspoken language of our heart. Psalm 147:5 declared, "Great is our Lord, and of great power: his understanding is infinite." God loves when we fellowship with Him. Imagine, in His Presence, we can take off the mask of who we think we are or who someone else says that we are and bare our souls before Him. It makes it so much easier when we do not have to 'dress it up' when we commune with our Father. Pretense goes out the window. A genuine heart to heart talk and a pouring out of the depth of our soul becomes the order of the moment or of the day. Don't let your spiritual menu be limited to talking to God about what concerns you, your family and others for whom the Holy Spirit prompts you to pray, but also thanking, praising, loving and worshiping Him for who He is. Paul said, "Giving thanks always for all things unto God and the Father in the name of our Lord Jesus Christ;" (Ephesians 5:20).

SET PRIORITIES

Put God first. We should not squeeze God in after we have finished everything else on our daily schedule. He wants to be first in our life. Our fellowship with God depends on our relationship with Him. If you have a good relationship with someone, you automatically want to spend quality and quantity time in his or her presence and have open and frequent communication. The Bible says, "If we say that we have fellowship with him, and walk in darkness, we lie, and do not the truth:" (I John 1:6). After we have cultivated a relationship with God, then we can build relationships with others. Surprisingly, on any plane believers and non-believers alike are crucial to move you along in your Christian walk. Employ every available opportunity to exercise spiritual aerobics — stretch and work all those muscles that have not been tested to see if we truly love unconditionally if someone speaks ill of us, cuts us off on the parkway, steps on our toes — unintentionally or intentionally. How would we react? Even if we don't respond with words, what does our body language say? Conversations are not limited to the words we speak. "Actions speak louder than words . . . "[3]

Prayer: Dear Heavenly Father, thank you for teaching me how to pray and to listen to your voice. Your instructions on how to begin and end my days are priceless and I am so appreciative that you love me enough to see that I make the best of the time that you give me each day. Father I ask that you sensitize my heart to the things that are dear to your heart that I may be a blessing to someone today in Jesus' name. Amen.

NOTES

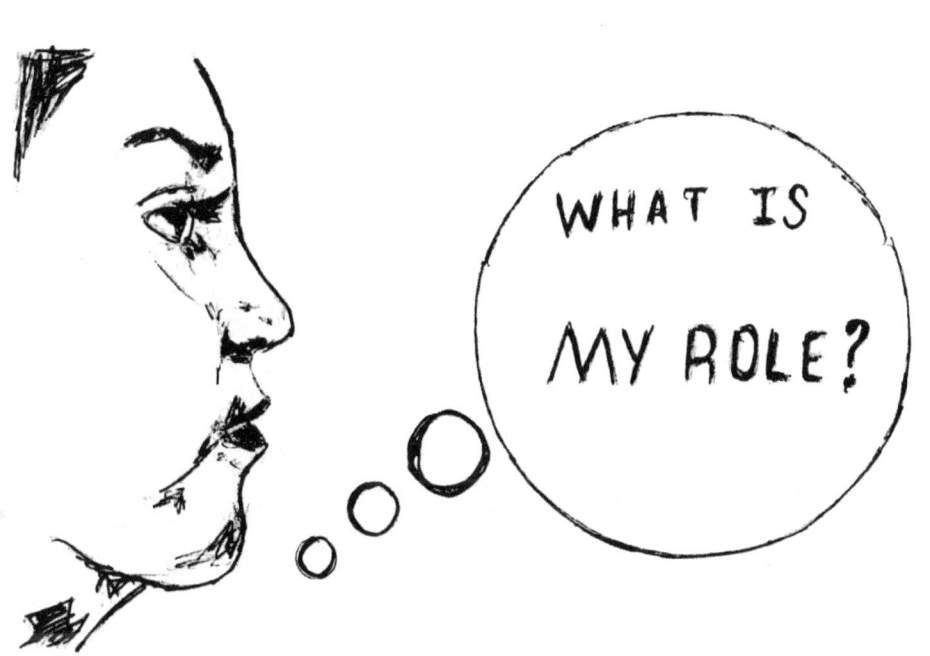

CHAPTER TWO

__The Believers Role in Prayer__

DAILY PRAYER

There are those of you, such as parents with a busy household, family, caregivers, etc., who due to abundant responsibilities, may feel that you don't have any more minutes nor any more energy left in your day. Even before your day begins you are already worn out and overwhelmed. You don't have a minute for yourself or a minute to think. So finding time to set aside for God seems impossible. You are most feverently yearning for time alone with Jesus! Call to remembrance the words that David said, "God is the LORD, which hath showed us light: bind the sacrifice with cords, even unto the horns of the altar" (Psalm 118:27). So it's not that you don't want to put God first, but all these things, responsibilities, and needs of others seem to convince you that there is no time for the most important person in your life. Look at what Jesus said to Martha:

Luke 10:38-42 (AMP)

38 Now while they were on their way, it occurred that Jesus entered a certain village, and a woman named Martha received and welcomed Him into her house.

39 And she had a sister named Mary, who seated herself at the Lord's feet and was listening to His teaching.

40 But Martha [overly occupied and too busy] was distracted with much serving; and she came up to Him and said, Lord, is it nothing to You that my sister has left me to serve alone? Tell her then to help me [to lend a hand and do her part along with me]!

41 But the Lord replied to her by saying, Martha, Martha, you are anxious and troubled about many things;

42 There is need of only one or but a few things. Mary has chosen the good portion [that which is to her advantage], which shall not be taken away from her.

Jesus reminded Martha that of all the things she needed to get done, time with Him is most important. Be encouraged! God sees and cares. He is very interested in our busy lives. David and Paul declared in these scriptures: "The eyes of the LORD are on the righteous, And His ears are open to their cry" (Psalm 34:15 NKJV). "And there is no creature hidden from His sight, but all things are naked and open to the eyes of Him to whom we must give account" (Hebrews 4:13 NKJV). Peter said, "For the eyes of the LORD are on the righteous, And His ears are open to their prayers; But the face of the Lord is against those who do evil" (I Peter 3:12 NKJV).

MARY LEE'S EXPRESSIONS

As a wife and mother of four very energetic children, I truly understand the demands of trying to "get it all done" while struggling to remain balanced and sane. You may think you are unable to set aside 10 or even 5 minutes to be quiet before Him. Let me offer a few suggestions that may help you. These are not hard and fast rules but just a few things to consider assisting you in getting started.

Throughout your day, as you go about your daily duties and activities, put a prayer and praise on your tongue. God will honor that. I Samuel 2:30b says, "...those who honor me I will honor, but those who despise me will be disdained" (NIV). Therefore, say what David said. "I will bless the LORD at all times; His praise shall continually be in my mouth" (Psalm 34:1 NKJV). The Scripture says, "Giving thanks always for all things to God the Father in the name of our Lord Jesus Christ," (Ephesians 5:20 NKJV).

Maintaining a routine is important as long as you are open to the leading of the Holy Spirit. If on any given day, He asks you to change your format you must be sensitive and obedient to His voice. For example, if you purpose to exercise physically everyday for 15 or 20 minutes and miss a day your body will let you know that you are off schedule. Your joints will stiffen up especially after you have been following a routine for several weeks or you may become sluggish or lose interest — heed the warning signs. Beware! The same is true when you neglect your spirit man by failing to read the Word of God or skipping devotion time. You become less fluent in your prayer flow and start searching for things to say because after a minute or two you have 'bottomed out', exhausted your prayer vocabulary — straining to make conversation with your Lord and Saviour. Communicating with your Father daily is the only way to keep your spiritual joints lubricated and your muscles toned. Willie frequently reminded us that, God is always ahead of time — never behind time. At any given time of the day or night "time stealers"[4] make other things seem more important or just take you away gradually from your focal point, which is prayer, and before you know it the day is gone.

DOROTHY JOHNSON'S PERSONALS

"Time stealers" are not always life or death situations. I am reminded of the time the Lord spoke three things to me during intercession several years before the birthing of this writing. The first thing God said was, "Don't be a thief of time." One might ask how does one become a thief of time? Think about it, time that you should be reading and studying the Word of God gets zapped by something else on your 'to do list.' This happens over and over again until there is no time to spend with God. Remember Willie's words, God is always ahead of time. I wish I could tell you that I began to make the best use of my time from that day forward. Unfortunately, that did not happen until circumstances drew me into the place that God had been calling me. It seems like I never had enough time. The time I planned in my head by making mental notes to work on this manuscript did not materialize because I did not have enough time. I allowed other things to steal my time day after day. I began to pray, Lord redeem the time that I may be able to set aside time to write. More than likely phrasing Mary, 'time stealers' are as Solomon declared, "the little foxes," whatever you allow to cause you to drift and be pulled away from a focal point (Song of Solomon 2:15). Jesus said, "And why call ye me, Lord, Lord, and do not the things which I say?" (Luke 6:46). It is easy to allow yourself to get side tracked by looking through papers, or as Mary says, permitting others to pull you into their situation for which you have no answer, or by just sitting idly by and letting your mind wander off into space.

This is what the Lord said to Mary during one of our family prayers:

Time Stealers

Begin to see the time stealers. With clarity you will begin to see the time stealers.
Good deeds are time stealers.
Well meaning friends are time stealers.
Worthy causes are time stealers.

Family and friends can be time stealers.
But is it what I asked you to do? It may look like a good thing. It may be worthy. But is it what I've asked you to do for this time? It may be the right thing. Just not the right time. The right people but not the right time.
Well meaning deeds can be time stealers.
But is it what I've asked you to do? Is it the right time to do it?
Somebody's emergency may not be my time. Don't step in my way. Compassion can be misplaced sometimes. Hindering the work of the Lord. Is it my time? Is it you to be my instrument for that time and purpose?
Sometimes it looks right but it's not my time. The devil uses the compassion of my people and their desire to do the right thing. But is it my time? Is it my time? Is it my place? Is it my person? For you to operate now?
Timing is everything. Sometimes you need to pray a little longer. Wait a little longer. Although it's somebody else's emergency it may not be my time. Jesus stayed a little bit longer when told Lazarus was dead. Somebody's emergency may not be my time. I am the Lord of time.
Begin to seek me about time. To investigate time, to study time. Timing and time.

There are time thieves and time stealers
Give me your time. I will redeem the time
I am the Lord of time
I AM TIME.
There is no time. I am eternal
I do not work on time
I create time
I bend time
I create and I end time
I begin and I end
I am the beginning and the end
All time is in me
I AM TIME
Time is a spiritual thing
Lord of time and space
I see all time
From end to beginning and back again
I am time
I am the Father of time
I break time
Time is in my hands

I hold time
I release time
I am time
I stretch time
I shortened time
I am time
I Am that I Am
From the beginning of time
From before time
I Am that I Am
I Am that I Am
I Am that I Am
Eternal, unchanging
I change time
I shift time
But I am unchanging
Because I Am time
See me as time
I master time
I do not work on man's time
I work on my time
I choose time
I release time and
I contain time
I fasten up time and
I release time
I don't hurry time
I have ordained My time
I move in time
I move outside of time
I made time and
I will end time
I am Lord of time
Speak in to time
Release your time to me
In the name of Jesus.
Start looking at time.
Discerning it in a different way.
In the name of Jesus.

The I Am
I Am
Look at time through the I Am
The I Am, hallelujah

CHALLENGES ALONG THE WAY

Prior to writing this book, some of us (sisters and brothers & brother-in-law) came together as a result of one brother in the prayer circle being attacked physically with stage 4 cancer in February 2012, the time he was diagnosed. We were geographically in different locations (Alabama, Kentucky, New Jersey, and New York). It began on a Sunday night March 11, 2012 when the Holy Spirit directed Willie to sound the alarm for family prayer. We settled on a time at 9:00 p.m. EST. As time progressed, Willie said "we need to write a prayer book for new believers." We were slow getting started. He continued to pressure us to put the pen to the paper. At the end of our Sunday night prayer and often throughout any given week, we would be expected to give a progress report. If we did not have anything to report, we felt the effect of unspoken words and purposed to go from nothing to something by the time the next week came around. As seasoned intercessors with the exception of one, our time in prayer was not just about our family. We prayed as the Holy Spirit directed us for pastors, youth, cities, states, nations, businesses, politicians, ministries and the list goes on.

When it comes to prayer you must always be in the ready, set, go position. Anything less than that is a set up for a detour that you will regret. Once you get off course, it takes time to get back to the place that you once were. Discipline is crucial to maintaining spiritual stride. If you are not careful, laziness will also creep in — so you have to stay plugged in to the Source, Jesus. Jesus said, "If ye abide in me, and my words abide in you, ye shall ask what ye will, and it shall be done unto you" (John 15:7).

DOROTHY'S PERSONALS

The second thing the Lord spoke to me during intercession was 'fortify'. God knew that I needed to build myself up in the Word to lend strong support during challenging times to others and to me. Some encounters we have in life require strength of body, mind, soul and spirit to withstand the grueling tests that come without a cheat sheet to get us through. Spiritual battles are won on our knees. There are no 'Cliffs Notes' to explain challenges and trials on this journey called life. The Holy Spirit helps us get through our hourly, daily, weekly, monthly and yearly ups and downs. He is the Interpreter of languages — naturally and spiritually that we do not understand. Paul admonishes us, "Likewise the Spirit also helps in our weaknesses. For we do not know what we should pray for as we ought, but the Spirit Himself makes intercession for us with groanings which cannot be uttered" (Romans 8:26 NKJV).

MARY'S EXPRESSIONS

When you are first awakening in the morning and before the concerns of the day overtake you, say something like "Thank you Lord. I love you Jesus. I give you this day. I praise you Lord for your goodness." It doesn't matter if your prayer may have different words. The important thing is to give God thanks and praises and put Him first over your day. As you continue to talk with Him about your concerns be sensitive to the leading of the Holy Spirit. He may lead you to pray in a way you have not planned nor understand. The reason for this change in direction may not be immediately forthcoming but be assured you will be blessed by your obedience. I Samuel 15:22 states, "…Has the Lord as much pleasure in your burnt offerings and sacrifices as in your obedience? Obedience is far better than sacrifice. He is much more interested in your listening to Him than in your offering the fat of rams to him" (TLB).

Many mornings this is my prayer. "Good morning Daddy, Papa, Abba. Good morning Jesus. Good morning Holy Spirit. Thank you Lord. Thank you Jesus. Thank you Holy Spirit. I praise you Lord. I thank you for Who you are. Thank you so much Father for loving me." It's just a simple prayer of love, thanksgiving, and praise. Many times, as I go on to pray about my concerns, I sense the presence of the Holy Spirit leading me in a different direction. When I yield my will to His I am always blessed and many times I feel light, refreshed, renewed, and strengthened.

Continuing my conversation with my Father is not limited to where I am. For example, while in the shower, between or even while yelling at the kids and/or your spouse to get moving, offer up thanksgiving and praise. Consider this from Psalm 118:24 "This is the day which the Lord hath made; we will rejoice and be glad in it." I like the way the Aramaic Bible in Plain English says it: "This is the day that Lord Jehovah has made; come, we will leap for joy and rejoice in him!" You may not want to leap just now but "calleth those things that be not as though they were!" (Romans 4:17)

DOROTHY'S PERSONALS

The third thing the Lord spoke to me was, "relentless intercession". I am not sure I know or even fully understand exactly what that means. Merriam-Webster's Dictionary defines 'relentless' as unrelenting, harsh; merciless; pitiless; unremitting, constant, never ending, unceasing, endless. I knew God was calling me to a deeper intensity of intercession and I am still on the road to that place where He wants me to be. Since that time, I have had a challenge and I would like to take this opportunity to share it with you. In May 2013, I went for my annual mammogram and received a letter that I needed to come for a follow up. That always raises concern. However, in recent times past, I had prayed that God would give me the grace to accept the doctors' report with praises to Him whether they determined it to be good or bad. I had to settle it in my spirit "whose report I would believe." I chose to believe the report of the Lord according to what Jesus said, "…If thou canst believe, all things are possible to him that believeth" (Mark 9:23). It turned out that after several tests the final results were in and before going for the last test, I felt an overwhelming peace. Yes, the results were that I had a small mass that was malignant. I needed a Word to stand on. During some quiet time with the Lord several years ago, the Lord said, "there are many Scriptures on healing; however, every healing Scripture is not for you." In other words we have to seek God for a Scripture to stand on for our particular situation. For this test, the Lord gave me Isaiah 54:17, "No weapon that is formed against thee shall prosper; and every tongue that shall rise against thee in judgment thou shalt condemn. This is the heritage of the servants of the LORD, and their righteousness is of me, saith the LORD."

The Amplified Version says it this way, "But no weapon that is formed against you shall prosper, and every tongue that shall rise against you in judgment you shall show to be in the wrong. This [peace, righteousness, security, triumph over opposition] is the heritage of the servants of the Lord [those in whom the ideal Servant of the Lord is reproduced]; this is the righteousness or the vindication which they obtain from Me [this is that which I impart to them as their justification], says the Lord."

In September 2013, I had a lumpectomy and am currently under the care of an Integrative Medicine Doctor, Kevin D. Holder, M.D. - Holistic Physician. (Name used by permission). My lifestyle has changed to say the least, both naturally and spiritually. Naturally through a healthy diet, regimented daily exercise, supplements for nutrient deficiency, Kangen's Ionized (alkaline)

Water, rest, and I am working on getting eight hours of sleep nightly and reducing the stress level in my busy schedule. The Lord also let me know that I can't do it (healing) by myself through diet alone. So, spiritually I strive to take in more of the Word, and acting on what God says about me in His Word; meditating on the goodness of the Lord, speaking the Word over my body, praising, worshiping and being thankful, as well as increased times of prayer and deeper intercession. Philippians 4:8 is one of my daily confessions, "Finally, brethren, whatsoever things are true, whatsoever things are honest, whatsoever things are just, whatsoever things are pure, whatsoever things are lovely, whatsoever things are of good report; if there be any virtue, and if there be any praise, think on these things." Worship is my passion. I live to be in the presence of the Lord. Hallelujah!

Trials were never meant to take us by surprise. God is speaking all the time. Are you listening? Since the Lord initially spoke to me about 'relentless intercession' and as He is teaching me day by day in my communion with Him, I think I am beginning to understand what it means. I have asked myself the question, could this have been avoided if I had been obedient to the voice of the Lord? Not sure — but I know that God wanted me to be prepared emotionally and spiritually for the punches that I would get along this stretch of the road. The Bible says, "That the trial of your faith, being much more precious than of gold that perisheth, though it be tried with fire, might be found unto praise and honour and glory at the appearing of Jesus Christ:" (1 Peter 1:7). I am so thankful for the strong bond of family and friends, my prayer warrior partners at 3:00 a.m. and 5:00 a.m. and at other times, and for my spiritual covering Bishop Hubert Banks, as well as other ministries that are a real blessing to me. The anointed praise and worship ministry of Israel Houghton and New Breed helps me position myself for time alone with the King. I am eternally grateful for these God-ordained connections that are still contributing deeply to my healing.

MARY'S EXPRESSIONS
Throughout your entire day, whether toiling over dirty dishes and housework, caring for a sick loved one, running errands, or running the boardroom, take a breath and breathe out a prayer to the Lord. Although it may not appear life threatening at first glance, let me assure you an overabundance of stress may cause mental and physical challenges and can even kill you! This is why I think David's words are appropriate here. "In my

distress [when seemingly closed in] I called upon the Lord and cried to my God; He heard my voice out of His temple (heavenly dwelling place), and my cry came before Him, into His [very] ears." (Psalm 18:6 AMP). Then remember this; "Shout for joy to the LORD, all the earth, burst into jubilant song with music;" (Psalm 98:4 NIV).

Things are happening in our lives all day everyday, which demand our attention. Sometimes the changes are sudden, while at other times they may be gradual. Nevertheless, changes are certain to come and we have to be prepared emotionally, psychologically and spiritually. Again, God will forewarn His children about attacks in advance giving us time to 'fortify'. We may miss the warning for various reasons (too busy, overcrowded schedules, listening for God to speak as He did in the past — that's called familiarity…). The Scripture says in 2 Kings 6:12, "And one of his servants said, 'None, my lord, O king; but E-li'-sha, the prophet who is in Israel, tells the king of Israel the words that you speak in your bedroom'" (NKJV). It can even be easy to talk yourself out of communicating with your Heavenly Father about things that we assess as being bothersome to God. Get it in your spirit; everything that concerns you concerns God because He loves you. Just like your earthly father can take one look at your face and tell that something is wrong without your uttering one word, so the God of your Salvation has a deeper love and concern for you. Your natural dad does not leave you to solve your own problem; instead he will ask you, "why are you sad?" Then he will do all that he can to ease your mind and steer you in the right direction because he loves you. The Scripture says, "If you then, being evil, know how to give good gifts to your children, how much more will your Father who is in heaven give good things to those who ask Him!" (Matthew 7:11 NKJV). Additionally, don't be shy about asking God for a prayer partner of like faith. It is important to have someone come in agreement with you in prayer. The Bible says, "…one chase a thousand, and two put ten thousand to flight…" (Deuteronomy 32:30). The Prophet Amos said, "Can two walk together except they be agreed?" (Amos 3:3).

Believers need to be strong. To keep from being a weakling in prayer, don't be tricked by distractions into having 'missed meals' of daily prayer. Your spiritual stomach will begin to growl. Communication is an important tool. That's how we build relationships that last by staying connected to the Vine. Jesus said, "I AM the true vine…" (John 15:1). If you were to skip days without talking to a friend or family member, all involved would feel the strain on the relationship and there would be a drifting apart. Start up the communication engine of 'casual talk,' and begin to reconnect with frequent contact. Make prayer a lifestyle not something that you squeeze in when you have a moment to spare or when you have a crisis. Spiritual idleness produces a slow start. It is impossible to go from zero to fifty in a split second under ordinary circumstances regardless of the method of transport used. Staying in the prayer mode is like being in the eye of the storm — calm and peaceful all the time. The Bible says, "Thou wilt keep him in perfect peace, whose mind is stayed on thee: because he trusteth in thee" (Isaiah 26:3).

As you continue to honor the Lord with your time by being in His presence there will be occasions when it may seem like you have been praying for an hour but upon checking the clock, it may only be five minutes. You will begin to realize that God has redeemed your time. The Epistle of Ephesians assures, "Making the most of every opportunity, because the days are evil" (Ephesians 5:16 NIV).

Hallelujah! All Praise to God! He is faithful! "Your faithfulness is from generation to generation; You have established the earth, and it stands fast" (Psalm 119:90 AMP). "Faithful is He Who is calling you [to Himself] and utterly trustworthy, and He will also do it [fulfill His call by hallowing and keeping you]" (I Thessalonians 5:24 AMP).

WEEKLY PRAYER

Set realistic goals before choosing a specific week. Will you be faithful to whatever week you choose? Commitment carries a price tag. Count the cost. Jesus said, "For which of you, intending to build a tower, sitteth not down first, and counteth the cost…" (Luke 14:28). Focus on what you want to accomplish in prayer. For example, praying for salvation of a family member, praying for your children, praying for your church or praying for your community. Distractions will come — sometimes with persistence.

Weekly praying should go beyond your daily prayer time. Praying with a prayer partner on a weekly basis will strengthen your spiritual base and help bring answers in situations that are more deeply rooted in the ditch of poverty (natural and/or spiritual) and require more digging to pull the roots out of the soil of unbelief, doubt and discouragement. This is only accomplished by declaring the Word of God consistently.

Jesus alone knows the true needs of His people. First and foremost — you should desire more endearing conversations with your Father, then ask Him to teach you how to listen so you can pray His heart about every prayer need. Even in personal prayers, do not hesitate to seek the Holy Spirit's guidance each time you go before the throne of God. In so doing, you will avoid unnecessary seasons of drought — a place of being stuck and becoming frustrated when you don't get answers right away.

Some prayer petitions or requests require more spiritual muscle. In Genesis 8:22, God talks about "seedtime and harvest — meaning '*seed + time = harvest*".[5] "While the earth remaineth, seedtime and harvest, and cold and heat, and summer and winter, and day and night shall not cease." Meditate on that truth for a while and your thinking will be revolutionized. The farmer applies that principle year after year when he plants a seed of corn, grain or wheat, etc. in the Spring and harvest it in late Summer or Fall. Some of us can personally relate to the 'farmer principle' having grown up in the South on a farm. At the end of the season when all the crops were harvested, the farmer had to save seed from each planting for the next season. He could not eat the seed that was set aside for planting the next year. Otherwise, he would have to buy or borrow from a neighbor and wait for two seasons to pass, the one he missed and the one in which he planted to bring forth a harvest. Believe me that would be a long time to wait for food to eat or grain to sell to meet the needs of the family. Growth is what God wants from His children. Peter declares, "As newborn babes, desire the sincere milk of the word, that ye may grow thereby:" (I Peter 2:2).

OTHER TIMES
Hezekiah

We grow in our prayer life when it is neither a burdensome chore to adhere to nor a prescribed legalistic act to perform. Rather it is an opportunity to impact the Kingdom and surrounding circumstances whether out of fulfillment or out of desperation as Hezekiah did in (2 Kings 20:1-3 AMP).

1. IN THOSE days Hezkiah became deadly ill. The prophet Isaiah son of Amoz came and said to him, Thus says the Lord: Set your house in order, for you shall die; you shall not recover.

2. Then Hezekiah turned his face to the wall, and prayed unto the Lord, saying,

3 I beseech You, O Lord, [earnestly] remember now how I have walked before You in faithfulness and truth and with a whole heart [entirely devoted to You] and have done what is good in Your sight. And Hezekiah wept bitterly.

    God heard the deep cry of Hez-e-ki'ah's heart and His Hand was moved in Hezekiah's direction when He told the prophet Isaiah to speak to Hezekiah the words as recorded in (II Kings 20:5, 6 ESV).

5 Turn back, and say to Hezekiah the leader of my people, Thus says the Lord, the God of David your father: I have heard your prayer; I have seen your tears. Behold, I will heal you. On the third day you shall go up to the house of the LORD,

6 and I will add fifteen years to your life. I will deliver you and this city out of the hand of the king of Assyria, and I will defend this city for my own sake and for my servant David's sake.

God will do the same for you in what you declare as good times, bad times and at any time what He did for Hezekiah. He longs to be good to His people. As a good Father, He takes pleasure in loading you with blessings throughout every day. David said, "Blessed be the Lord, who daily loadeth us with benefits, even the God of our salvation" (Psalm 68:19).

Other requirements in Scripture directed Hannah to pray in I Samuel.

I Samuel 1:1-28

1 NOW there was a certain man of Ra-ma-tha'-im-zophim, of mount E'phra-im, and his name was El-ka'nah, the son of Je-ro'-ham, the son of E-li'-hu, the son of Tuhu, the son of Zuph, an Eph'-ra'thite:

2 And he had two wives; the name of the one was Hannah, and the name of the other Pe- nin'-nah: and Peninnah had children, but Hannah had no children.

3 And this man went up out of his city yearly to worship and to sacrifice unto the LORD of hosts in Shiloh. And the two sons of Eli, Hoph'-ni and Phin'-e'has, the priests of the LORD, were there.

4 And when the time was that El-ka'-nah offered, he gave to Pe-nin'-nah his wife, and to all her sons and her daughters, portions:

5 But unto Hannah he gave a worthy portion; for he loved Hannah: but the LORD had shut up her womb.

6 And her adversary also provoked her sore, for to make her fret, because the LORD had shut up her womb.

7 And as he did so year by year, when she went up to the house of the LORD, so she provoked her; therefore she wept, and did not eat.

8 Then said El'ka'-nah her husband to her, Hannah, why weepest thou? And why eatest thou not? And why is thy heart grieved? Am not I better to thee than ten sons?

9 So Hannah rose up after they had eaten in Shiloh, and after they had drunk. Now Eli the priest sat upon a seat by a post of the temple of the LORD.

10 And she was in bitterness of soul, and prayed unto the LORD, and wept sore.

11 And she vowed a vow, and said, O LORD of hosts, if thou wilt indeed look on the affliction of thine handmaid, and remember me, and not forget thine handmaid, but wilt give unto thine handmaid a man child, then I will give him unto the LORD all the days of his life, and there shall no razor come upon his head.

12 And it came to pass, as she continued praying before the LORD, that Eli marked her mouth.

13 Now Hannah, she spake in her heart; only her lips moved, but her voice was not heard: therefore Eli thought she had been drunken.

14 And Eli said unto her, How long wilt thou be drunken? Put away thy wine from thee.

15 And Hannah answered and said, No, my lord, I am a woman of a sorrowful spirit: I have drunk neither wine nor strong drink, but have poured out my soul before the LORD.

16 Count not thine handmaid for a daughter of Be'-li-al: for out of the abundance of my complaint and grief have I spoken hitherto.

17 Then Eli answered and said, Go in peace: and the God of Israel grant thee thy petition that thou hast asked of him.

18 And she said, Let thine handmaid find grace in thy sight. So the woman went her way, and did eat, and her countenance was no more sad.

19 And they rose up in the morning early, and worshipped before the LORD, and returned, and came to their house to Ramah: and El-ka'-nah knew Hannah his wife; and the LORD remembered her.

20 Wherefore it came to pass, when the time was come about after Hannah had conceived, that she bare a son, and called his name Samuel, saying, Because I have asked him of the LORD.

21 And the man El-ka'-nah, and all his house, went up to offer unto the LORD the yearly sacrifice, and his vow.

22 But Hannah went not up; for she said unto her husband, I will not go up until the child be weaned, and then I will bring him, that he may appear before the LORD, and there abide for ever.

23 And El-ka'-nah her husband said unto her, Do what seemeth thee good; tarry until thou have weaned him; only the LORD establish his word. So the woman abode, and gave her son suck until she weaned him.

24 And when she had weaned him, she took him up with her, with three bullocks, and one e'phah of flour, and a bottle of wine, and brought him unto the house of the LORD in Shiloh: and the child was young.

25 And they slew a bullock, and brought the child to Eli.

26 And she said, Oh my lord, as thy soul liveth, my lord, I am the woman that stood by thee here, praying unto the LORD.

27 For this child I prayed; and the LORD hath given me my petition which I asked of him:

28 Therefore also I have lent him to the LORD; as long as he liveth he shall be lent to the LORD. And he worshipped the LORD there.

The Prophet Daniel

Prayer also establishes a bond between the Giver/Creator of life and the recipient/child of God through all circumstances. No one exhibited the relevance and value of this relationship more than the Prophet Daniel. Daniel understood the link between he and God was more important than that between mankind and the dictates of man's law, especially when man's law was in opposition to a connection with God. Even after an established decree to petition no other authority than the king or risk death Daniel did not waiver. The Bible says, "Now when Daniel knew that the writing was signed, he went into his house; and his windows being open in his chamber toward Jerusalem, he kneeled upon his knees three times a day, and prayed, and gave thanks before his God, as he did aforetime" (Daniel 6:10). Daniel's continued prayer was not merely to defy the king. Daniel and King Darius had a strong bond of mutual respect and admiration for one another. In fact the king had made Daniel the first of three presidents over the entire kingdom. But he realized there was a higher power that controlled all circumstances. That realization compelled him to prayer no matter what, so the prophet clung to his source.

We must understand that God is the source of all wisdom and knowledge and that he wants to give good things according to His will. As He equipped Solomon with wisdom we also need this gift, especially when deceit runs rampant on the Earth. James said, "If any of you lack wisdom, let him ask of God, that giveth to all men liberally, and upbraideth not; and it shall be given him" (James 1:5).

Prayer: Jesus I thank you for the personal connection and relationship that I have with you through prayer. I thank you that it is a doorway that is always open and as a believer I am never denied access. As I go about my daily life may I incorporate this time and realize that it is one of the most valuable periods of my daily walk with you. My prayer time will be sacred, focused and intentional. Teach me to lift up those around me who are in need in Jesus' name. Amen.

NOTES

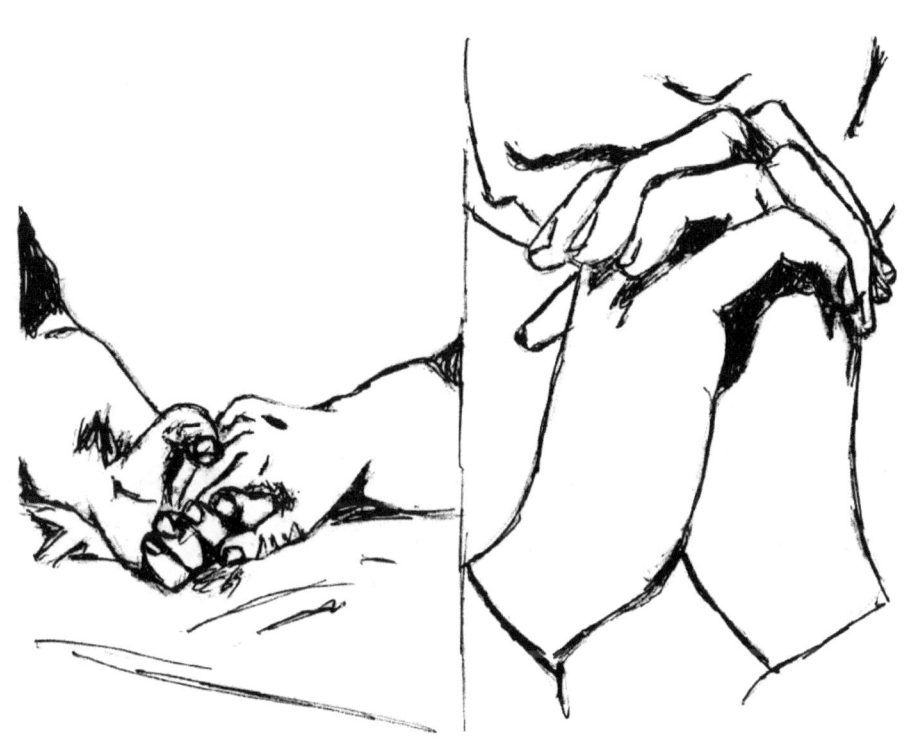

CHAPTER THREE

How to Pray Individually or Corporately?

CHOOSE A TIME - FOR DAILY PRAYER

Choosing a time for prayer is of utmost importance because it requires discipline. You want to be committed and faithful. After all you are meeting with the King of kings — don't take it lightly. You are royalty. Think about what would work for you not just for the moment but in the long run as the days become weeks and the weeks become months and yes, the months become years and even beyond that. Because prayer is having a conversation with God, it is a lifetime journey and should be viewed everyday with great expectancy and anticipation. One should take great care in selecting a time to spend with God. It should be the most important time of each day. Preparing to meet with God is vital. David said, "FOR GOD alone my soul waits in silence; from Him comes my salvation" (Psalm 62:1 AMP). Take note of the word preparing. Webster's Dictionary defines prepare as to make ready beforehand. To put things or oneself in readiness; make preparations. Meeting with God means to prepare your heart; repent of any and all sin in thought, word or deed. Prepare your soul; the person that you are, character, personality and conscious. Prepare your body by getting a sufficient amount of rest, exercise and proper nutrition. Posture yourself for this precious time in the throne room by taking action that moves you from the natural to the spiritual.

It may be necessary to quiet your spirit and calm your emotions so that the distractions are minimal to none. What does it mean to quiet your spirit? There are several things one could do; just to name a few, you could begin with writing down all the things that are bombarding your mind — the grocery list, the school activities, children, homework, house chores, gardening, returning phone calls, community activities, church duties and the list goes on. Once you have taken a few minutes to list the most important time stealers emphasized by Mary, then you can center on bringing your emotional stress level into a place of rest and peace — uninterrupted time with God. Your time with God is special. If you are having a conversation with someone and are constantly interrupted, it's annoying to say the least, and you may end up suggesting a more convenient time when you can give your undivided attention to the conversation. God expects to meet with you at the appointed time that you designate and when the course is clear because it will be a time for two — you and God. Choose wisely and prayerfully. David revealed his heart when he said, "The one thing I want from God, the thing I seek most of all, is the privilege of meditating in his Temple, living in his presence every day of my life, delighting in his incomparable perfections and glory" (Psalm 27:4 TLB).

However, there are circumstances that prevail when choosing a prayer schedule. It may not be as easy when one has a family. Mary writes to encourage those who have to adjust schedules in order to fulfill spousal and parental duties.

MARY'S INSPIRATIONS

The many demands of my life too often dictate my schedule. This makes finding a regularly scheduled time for prayer quite the challenge, but not impossible. The Gospel of Luke declares, "For with God nothing will be impossible" (1:37 NKJV). I had to learn to be flexible and follow the leading of the Holy Spirit. David said in Psalm 143:10, "And teach me to do your pleasure, because you are my God; your Spirit is sweet; you will lead me in the way of life" (Aramaic Bible in Plain English). The CJB version renders the last part of this verse like this; "…Let your good Spirit guide me on ground that is level."

When my children were younger they had an early bedtime. After all were in bed and the house was settled and quiet, I'd breathe a deep sigh of relief and freedom and rush to my oasis on the living room couch. One definition of oasis, as defined by dictionary.reference.com is: "something serving as a refuge, relief, or pleasant change from what is usual, annoying, difficult, etc." No matter how much we may love and enjoy what we do, who we are or who we are with, there are times when we need to be alone with our refuge, Jesus. David said, "You are a hiding place for me; You, Lord, preserve me from trouble, You surround me with songs and shouts of deliverance…" (Psalm 32:7 AMP).

Sometimes I'd go straight into praise and prayer. Other times I would just enjoy the silence, peace, and rest, allowing the Holy Spirit to lead me into a natural flow of praise and prayer while basking in His Presence. As the children grew and began to manage their own bedtimes, I found I needed to change also. I began to rise before dawn to meet with the Lord. David proclaimed, "My voice you shall hear in the morning, O LORD; In the morning I will direct it to You, And I will look up" (Psalm 5:3 NKJV).

Through the passage of time and family dynamics, I would again have to change my prayer time. After the chaos of morning preparation and everyone was finally out of the house I would then try to get before the Lord. I say try because this particular schedule was the most challenging and the most difficult to maintain with any consistency. Once my day shifts into busyness, many times it is difficult for me to make that transition back again to quietness. Therefore, most times I found it very hard to discipline myself enough to refocus and quiet my mind after all the morning activity. Another thing is that my brain kept bumping into the list of household duties, meetings, appointments, and all the things that I had scheduled to get accomplished. Thirdly, it seemed by eight a.m. the phone would begin to ring with an endless list of friends, solicitors, businesses, and whoever else, calling. Finally, what was most discouraging was that even when I did manage to get quiet before the Lord, frequently, I would allow the weight of that list of responsibilities to pressure me into shortening my time with Him. But, even though I failed many times in my attempts to be consistent, and had to routinely renounce the lies of condemnation from the devil, I never completely gave up, but had to surrender the realities of interruptions to the Lord. I would remind myself of the faithfulness of my Father that's recorded in:

Lamentations 3:21-24 AMP

21 But this I recall and therefore have I hope and expectation:

22 It is because of the Lord's mercy and loving-kindness that we are not consumed, because His [tender] compassions fail not.

23 They are new every morning; great and abundant is Your stability and faithfulness.

24 The Lord is my portion or share, says my living being (my inner self); therefore will I hope in Him and wait expectantly for Him.

At this stage in my life my individual prayer time is mainly in the morning, but I speak with Him throughout my day. Through my journey I am learning to trust the Lord more and to not only follow His leading but to be swift to do so. In spite of all that I try to do to make it work, the realization is that I am still a work in progress. Thank you Lord.

There were times when, things did not run smoothly and I'd throw up my hands in frustration at some unplanned and unwelcome interruption. There were also times when it was difficult to refocus and times when I was unsuccessful to do so. But with the Lord's help I persevered. The enemy is always looking to disrupt your communication with the Lord. John 10:10 TLB says, "The thief's purpose is to steal, kill and destroy. My purpose is to give you life in all its fullness." So keep going. Don't quit. The proper way for Christians to conduct themselves is found in II Thessalonians 3:13 (AMP). So it is appropriate to use it here as encouragement to "…not become weary or lose heart in doing right [but continue in well-doing without weakening]. The CJB says, "…don't slack off!" In Romans 8:26a (TLB) the Scripture tells us we have a helper who will cause us to succeed if we just don't quit!

SELECT DURATION

Start slow — 5 minutes, 10 minutes, 15 minutes, etc., increase and build as you go and grow in expanding your prayer vocabulary and build up your relationship, which will become natural as you develop in fellowshipping with God. The Bible says, "And beside this, giving all diligence, add to your faith virtue; and to virtue knowledge;" (II Peter 1:5). The Holy Spirit will begin to give you words to pray as your spirit is **watered** with the Word daily. You will ask yourself the question repeatedly; must this fellowship with my Saviour end? It will seem like the minutes have become hours and they will keep expanding as you seek more of the God who longs to fellowship and desires to have a relationship with you. Sometimes it is hard to grasp that God Almighty, the One who has all creation at His disposal, wants to spend time with you and me.

Unlike the corporate world and other segments of society where the space of the CEO (Chief Executive Officer) is off limits to the vast majority of employees, you, "child of God"[6] do not have to make an appointment when you want to have a conversation with your Heavenly Father. He is always available; never too busy to hear what is on your heart. Matter of fact, God loves when we talk to Him. What an honor and a privilege. This is how Isaiah assures us what God thinks when we come to Him, "Incline your ear, and come to Me. Hear, and your soul shall live; And I will make an everlasting covenant with you — The sure mercies of David" (Isaiah 55:3 NKJV).

BEGIN WITH A SCRIPTURE

The Word of God is to be the basis for all that you do for the Kingdom. You need the Word for understanding, guidance and wisdom to orchestrate the affairs of your life. The Holy Spirit will direct you to the right Scripture that speaks to where you are at any given moment. You could start by asking, Father where do you want me to begin in your Word today? Comfort is found in these words, "In all your ways acknowledge Him, And He shall direct your paths (Proverbs 3:6 NKJV). Then you listen for His still quiet voice to tell you where to go and when to stop. You may ask, how do I know God is telling me to read a certain Scripture? You will know by a "prompting or a knowing"[7] in your spirit and even as you turn the pages slowly and quietly, you will feel drawn to a certain passage of Scripture, which you may or may not understand at the moment. However, as the day progresses and you encounter the day's events you may know that God spoke to you and directed you to read that particular Word. The Gospel of John records, "He who is of God hears God's words; therefore you do not hear, because you are not of God" (John 8:47 NKJV).

In the developmental stages of your relationship with the Lord, you may not be sensitive enough to know His voice, but as you grow God's voice will become more recognizable. A word of caution, you do not want to get to the place of familiarity — meaning that you always know when God is speaking because you expect Him to speak to you as in times past. For example, God may have a friend call and tell you to take an alternate route home after work or school. On another occasion, you may get this strong feeling deep on the inside telling you to use a different path to your destination. There are numerous other ways that God could speak — it's a learning process as you commune with Him daily. God wants us to trust Him and walk close enough with Him to know His still small voice. Elijah is a witness to the quietness of God's voice in I Kings 19:12, which states, "And after the earthquake a fire; but the LORD was not in the fire: and after the fire a still small voice."

CHOOSE A DAY - FOR WEEKLY PRAYER

Decisions and choices — we all make them. Choosing a day for weekly prayer requires one to think it through because you have to consider others that may be praying with you. Could it be the beginning of a week, mid-week or at the end of the week? The time of day must also be taken into consideration. Sort through your mind and schedule to see if early in the day, mid day or late day would be a good time. Come together with other **pray-ers** and discuss the days and times to be considered, and then if it's agreeable to all, set that day and time to go before the Lord. David shows us how by these words, "Cause me to hear thy lovingkindness in the morning; for in thee do I trust: cause me to know the way wherein I should walk; for I lift up my soul unto thee" (Psalm 143:8).

ALONE WITH GOD - MEDITATION

Decide what works best for you. When you want to read a book or just meditate, you do not want to be in a busy environment with lots of traffic, children, pets or other disturbances. A secluded place in the house — out of obvious sight of others is most desirable; sitting or reclining in a chaise lounge in the yard shielded by shrubbery or some other nook in or outside of the house where you are not visible would serve as the perfect place to tune in to God and tune out the clanging and banging of everyday life. The Bible says, "…Come ye yourselves apart into a desert place, and rest awhile: for there were many coming and going, and they had no leisure so much as to eat" (Mark 6:31). Finding time to be alone with the Lord is absolutely imperative! But, for some of you, right now, it may be impossible to go to an actual physical place of seclusion with God. So, until that occasion comes when you can physically move yourself to such a place, ask the Lord for grace to get alone with Him mentally. Ask Him to teach you how to shut out the surrounding activity and noise. At one time or another all of us have "zoned out" and taken a "mental break" from what is going on around us. So take a mental break and spend some time with the Lord. You may even be able to relate or find inspiration in Susanna Wesley's Prayer Apron-Powerful Life Story (Sharon Glasgow) of fulfilling her commitment to the Lord. "She and her husband had 10 children that lived out of 19 birthed, and two of the children had challenges. Susanna struggled to find a secret place to get away with God. So she advised her children that when they saw her with her apron over her head, that meant she was in prayer and couldn't be disturbed."[8] What a **stimulating** witness to perseverance!

ESTABLISH A PRAYER ALTAR

First let's define 'altar.' It is a place where one comes to bow down, lie prostrate, kneel, stand, sit, or any other position where you can connect with God Almighty. A place where you are free to worship, praise, dance, jump, shout and rejoice, or just sit quietly in God's presence. It is a sacred place to offer the sacrifices of the fruit of your lips — alone **behind the veil**. Throughout Scripture, great men and women of God established altars and offered sacrifices to God as stated in the following Scriptures:

Genesis 8:20 (NKJV)
"Then Noah built an altar to the LORD, and took of every clean animal and of every clean bird, and offered burnt offerings on the altar."

Exodus 17:15 (NKJV)
"And Moses built an altar and called its name, The-LORD-Is-My-Banner;"

Luke 2:36, 37

36 And there was one Anna, a prophetess, the daughter of Pha-nu'-el, of the tribe of Aser: she was of a great age, and had lived with an husband seven years from her virginity;

37 And she was a widow of about fourscore and four years, which departed not from the temple, but served God with fastings and prayers night and day.

DOROTHY'S PERSONALS

Some years ago during my prayer time, I heard the Lord speak to me in my spirit, "build me an altar." In the beginning, I was unsure of what the Lord was saying, however, by the enlightenment of the Holy Spirit I received **revelation**. God wanted me to build Him an altar of praise. I have never regretted that day. What's good about that is the altar can be built beyond your designated devotional time. You can make it happen at anytime — while shopping, driving, taking a stroll in the park or during your exercise time at the gym. Learn to practice and cultivate the Presence of God. I am still learning and each day becomes more intimate.

DIFFERENT LOCATIONS

We live in a world that is vast and varied in climate, culture, time zones, etc. This difference should not become a barrier when it comes to linking with others in various parts of the world. We do not have to necessarily pray on the phone. The awakening hour in the USA may be the sleeping hour in Africa, Sweden, Israel or India so we are not to allow 'time' to set a trap for us. We only use time as a reference point as Willie aptly stated. We can still pray as one but not at the same time as it relates to a time clock. "God made time but is not controlled by time because He lives in eternity."[9] In Psalm 90:4 the Bible says, "For a thousand years in thy sight are but as yesterday when it is past, and as a watch in the night." We must elevate our thinking to a higher level by thinking like God thinks. II Peter 1:3 says, "According as his divine power hath given unto us all things that pertain unto life and godliness, through the knowledge of him that hath called us to glory and virtue:"

Knowing that we live in God, and that He dwells inside of us, our prayers on planet earth are heard in Heaven and He answers. We are in this place in the realm of time; God exists where time is not the issue, so praying with others who may be in a different time zone does not hinder spiritual movement to an Almighty God if the pray-ers align with His Word. They will bring forth results no matter the hour or location. Praying to Almighty God gets results. The Scripture according to the Gospel of Matthew Chapter 6 (NKJV) says, "when you pray" (verse 5a), not if you pray but "when you pray" (verse 6a) is the condition to seeing the hand of God move in the lives of people for His Kingdom business and for our individual lives.

Prayer: God you have allowed us the privilege to perform an act distinct from all the rest of your creation. The distinction of the gift of prayer permits us individually or corporately to link for a united purpose. Because of this sacred opportunity we thank you that there are no physical boundaries that can stop our interaction with you. As we pray with other believers teach us to magnify the impact of our prayers by being in agreement for the cause we are petitioning for and the results we are expecting in Jesus' name. Amen.

NOTES

CHAPTER FOUR

Preparation for Prayer and Intercession

STAGES

Before starting the prayer/intercession group it's important to seek God's direction. The Bible instructs us to, "Lean on, trust in, and be confident in the Lord with all your heart and mind and do not rely on your own insight or understanding" (Proverbs 3:5 AMP). Every work of the Lord should start with Him at the center. Spend time just being with Him, reading the Word, praying, praising, and worshipping. Find out what He thinks about it; get confirmation and His instruction on how to proceed. Find comfort in this Biblical truth, "If you want to know what God wants you to do, ask him, and he will gladly tell you, for he is always ready to give a bountiful supply of wisdom to all who ask him; he will not resent it" (James 1:5 TLB).

If you don't already know, ask the Lord who is to participate in the group. Then pray together and individually about how the group should proceed. Some things you may want to pray about are the purpose, focus, and length of time the group is to be maintained. Is the group only meeting for a specific length of time and praying about a specific issue or need?

Prayerfully decide when to meet, where to meet, what time to meet, and how to proceed. For example, if geographical location is an issue, try being creative. Today's technological advances offer a variety of options such as: by phone, Skype, face time, Linkedin, Twitter, etc.

Also, as you enter into this prayer/intercession commitment, it is important to begin where you are personally in your relationship and prayer life with the Lord. Although it's fine to use pointers from someone you may think is a "spiritual giant," don't completely mimic their behavior. Don't try to wear somebody else's armor. Before David became King he had to deal with a similar situation in I Samuel 17:38-39: (NKJV)

38 So Saul clothed David with his armor, and he put a bronze helmet on his head; he also clothed him with a coat of mail.

39 And David fastened his sword to his armor, and he tried to walk, for he had not tested them. And David said to Saul, "I cannot walk with these, for I have not tested them." So David took them off.

David was not used to wearing armor and was not yet prepared at this stage of his life and maturity to do so.

Intellectual and spiritual growth should continue until we meet Jesus. So, as you continue to grow in your relationship with the Lord, your prayers will mature like a child who grows through stages of development from a baby to adulthood, maturing not only physically but also mentally, emotionally, and spiritually. Before you begin to pray choose a place of comfort, avoid being stressed out before your time to be **stretched out**. Count the cost — short-term as opposed to long-term requirements of any endeavor is different. For example going on a trip for a day would require less preparation than going on a trip for a week or more. The longer the trip, the more water, food, money, etc. would be necessary for the journey. Once you embark on a prayer journey, one hour, one day or three days, one has to be trained in all of the start up modes (mental, emotional, spiritual, etc.) to be effective in communication with God at any level.

You might ask yourself the question, how can I be stressed out in prayer or intercession? Every phase of life requires one to spend time preparing and continuing to practice to keep stride with changes that are unavoidable (i.e. periods of growth, discipline, development, learning, hearing, confessing, etc.). There will also be times of stagnation and isolation and yes, not hearing from God because of **static** issues — not because God has stopped speaking necessarily. Learn to embrace these training tools and permit them to cultivate your moral fiber into a tapestry worthy of helping others, first on a personal level, and with the ultimate goal of expanding into a broader base.

It is important to understand that barriers will arise as we strive to **integrate** prayer or intercession into the routine — our life. These barriers will be displayed through different facets. In the natural world static causes interference to hearing because multiple frequencies of sound waves destructively interact with one another. The resulting effect is the lack of a clear and **concise** signal that can be audibly detected. During times of prayer a similar outcome can occur in the spiritual world. This static may be driven by the bombarding of our minds with negative thoughts from "signals" such as world's calamities or the attempt of Satan himself infiltrating our thought life. Thoughts of personal **inadequacy** may keep us from understanding that as believers we have full access to God through Christ. Sometimes we believe it is our duty to carry burdens that only Christ Himself can shoulder.

These prevailing feelings can plant the seed of deception that the Lord does not hear us and does not want to commune with us. As we learn more of the Lord and His ways we grow to understand and overcome the barriers that try to impede us, and the nature of the charter to which we are called. The following Scripture reinforces the tools that we need to perform our assigned tasks:

Romans 12:2
"And be not conformed to this world: but be ye transformed by the renewing of your mind, that ye may prove what is that good, and acceptable, and perfect, will of God."

Isaiah 59:16
"And he saw that there was no man, and wondered that there was no intercessor: therefore his arm brought salvation unto him; and his righteousness, it sustained him."

A prayer can be spoken at any given time because God is always available. God is not bound by space or time as declared in Psalm 121:4, "Behold, he that keepeth Israel shall neither slumber nor sleep." Instantaneous events such as an accident may require the need to pray for immediate results. But most often we can allot for planning time alone with God specifically for the purpose of prayer. Prayer is a sacred time that merits special attention. Understand that because this period is special you need to be intentional about committing to it. This form of prayer should be routine but not **ritualistic** - that is based more on the desire for a relationship rather than a prescribed performance that can lead to **legalism**. As believers, prayer should be as normal a commitment in our lives as the activities we perform on a daily basis.

We should be encouraged as we prepare for this activity that we are being allowed to commune with the Creator of all mankind and the universe! This very act takes us from the **mundane** to the Supernatural. Just as we prepare ourselves to meet earthly dignitaries likewise we should prepare to meet the highest Dignitary — the King above all kings.

Some key points to remember are:
Always find a place that will allow for prayer without interference. That place may be a literal closet, a car, or some other place that will reduce **sensitivity** to our natural senses and heighten our spiritual senses. Jesus himself went alone to pray.

Matthew 14:23 (NKJV)
And when He had sent the multitudes away, He went up on a mountain by Himself to pray. And when evening had come, He was alone there.

Matthew 26:39-42 (NKJV)
39 He went a little farther, and fell on his face, and prayed, saying, "O My Father, if it be possible, let this cup pass from Me; nevertheless, not as I will, but as You will."

40 Then He came to the disciples and found them asleep, and said to Peter, "What, could you not watch with Me one hour?

41 Watch and pray, lest you enter into temptation. The spirit indeed is willing, but the flesh is weak.

42 Again, a second time, He went away and prayed, saying, "O My Father, if this cup cannot pass away from Me unless I drink it, Your will be done."

Prayer does change things. We prepare to pray with an air of expectancy because Jesus' sacrifice allows it.

Hebrews 4:15, 16
15 For we have not an high priest which cannot be touched with the feeling of our infirmities; but was in all points tempted like as we are, yet without sin.

16 Let us therefore come boldly unto the throne of grace, that we may obtain mercy, and find grace to help in time of need.

James 4:1-3
1 FROM whence come wars and fightings among you? come they not hence, even of your lusts that war in your members?

2   Ye lust, and have not: ye kill, and desire to have, and cannot obtain: ye fight and war, yet ye have not, because ye ask not.

3   Ye ask, and receive not, because ye ask amiss, that ye may consume it upon your lusts.

There is always a need for prayer because there will always be challenges and needs in the world. But ultimately there is always victory!

John 16:33

These things I have spoken unto you, that in me ye might have peace. In the world ye shall have tribulation: but be of good cheer; I have overcome the world.

Our Creator is not distracted or irritated by our petitions to Him. In fact we are admonished to pray.

Luke 18:1

AND he spake a parable unto them to this end, that men ought always to pray, and not to faint;

Everything in this earth realm begins with a starting place, point or position that can sometimes be laborious. One thing to keep in mind is that you can never reach the end of anything unless you start at something.

***Prayer:** Dear Heavenly Father, thank you for the desire to expand in prayer and to pray for others while receiving personal strength and encouragement. Thank you for teaching me how to talk to you as a friend and as my Lord and Saviour Jesus Christ because you made it all possible at Calvary. Today I look forward to meeting with you in Jesus' name. Amen.*

NOTES

RIDDLE

Proverbs 30:15b

There are three things that are
never satisfied, yea, four things
say not, It is enough

CHAPTER FIVE

Making the Transition from Prayer to Intercession

We may start our prayer thanking God for who He is and for the opportunity to call on Him as our Source of supply as Philippians 4:4 says, "Always be full of joy in the Lord; I say it again, rejoice!" (TLB). During this time of personal interaction with God an urge may come to pray for someone other than one's self. Intercession is a prayer offered up for others. The prayer may be rendered for a person or group of people. Intercession can be for those we know or don't know. Some examples of intercession in the Bible are:

Moses praying on behalf of his kinsmen after they turned away from God:

Exodus 32:11-14 (NKJV)

11 Then Moses pleaded with the LORD his God, and said: "LORD, why does Your wrath burn hot against Your people whom You have brought out of the land of Egypt with great power and with a mighty hand?

12 "Why should the Egyptians speak, and say, 'He brought them out to harm them, to kill them in the mountains, and to consume them from the face of the earth'? Turn from Your fierce wrath, and relent from this harm to Your people.

13 "Remember Abraham, Isaac, and Israel, Your servants, to whom You swore by Your own self, and said to them, 'I will multiply your descendants as the stars of heaven; and all this land that I have spoken of I give to your descendants, and they shall inherit it forever.'"

14 So the LORD relented from the harm which He said He would do to His people.

Daniel praying on behalf of the captive Israelites:

Daniel 9:3-19 (NKJV)

3 Then I set my face toward the Lord God to make request by prayer and

supplications, with fasting, sackcloth, and ashes.

4 And I prayed to the LORD my God, and made confession, and said, "O Lord, great and awesome God, who keeps His covenant and mercy with those who love Him, and with those who keep His commandments,

5 "we have sinned and committed iniquity, we have done wickedly and rebelled, even by departing from Your precepts and Your judgments.

6 "Neither have we heeded Your servants the prophets, who spoke in Your name to our kings and our princes, to our fathers and all the people of the land.

7 "O Lord, righteousness belongs to You, but to us shame of face, as it is this day — to the men of Judah, to the inhabitants of Jerusalem and all Israel, those near and those far off in all the countries to which You have driven them, because of the unfaithfulness which they have committed against You.

8 "O Lord, to us belongs shame of face, to our kings, our princes, and our fathers, because we have sinned against You.

9 "To the Lord our God belong mercy and forgiveness, though we have rebelled against Him.

10 "We have not obeyed the voice of the LORD our God, to walk in His laws, which He set before us by His servants the prophets.

11 "Yes, all Israel has transgressed Your law, and has departed so as not to obey Your voice; therefore the curse and the oath written in the Law of Moses the servant of God have been poured out on us, because we have sinned against Him.

12 "And He has confirmed His words, which He spoke against us and against our judges who judged us, by bringing upon us a great disaster; for under the whole heaven such has never been done as what has been done to Jerusalem.

13 "As it is written in the Law of Moses, all this disaster has come upon us;

yet we have not made our prayer before the LORD our God, that we might turn from our iniquities and understand Your truth.

14 "Therefore the LORD has kept the disaster in mind, and brought it upon us; for the LORD our God is righteous in all the works which He does, though we have not obeyed His voice.

15 "And now, O Lord, our God, who brought Your people out of the land of Egypt with a mighty hand, and made Yourself a name, as it is this day — we have sinned, we have done wickedly!

16 "O Lord, according to all Your righteousness, I pray, let Your anger and Your fury be turned away from Your city Jerusalem, Your holy mountain; because for our sins, and for the iniquities of our fathers, Jerusalem and Your people have become a reproach to all who are around us.

17 "Now therefore, our God, hear the prayer of Your servant, and his supplications, and for the Lord's sake cause Your face to shine on Your sanctuary, which is desolate.

18 "O my God, incline Your ear and hear; open Your eyes and see our desolations, and the city which is called by Your name; for we do not present our supplications before You because of our righteous deeds, but because of Your great mercies.

19 "O Lord, hear! O Lord, forgive! O Lord, listen and act! Do not delay for Your own sake, my God, for Your city and Your people are called by Your name."

Jesus, the consummate intercessor praying for His disciples and all believers:

Matthew 17:6-26 (NKJV)

6 And when the disciples heard it, they fell on their faces and were greatly afraid.

7 But Jesus came and touched them and said, "Arise, and do not be afraid."

8 When they had lifted up their eyes, they saw no one but Jesus only.

9   Now as they came down from the mountain, Jesus commanded them, saying, "Tell the vision to no one until the Son of Man is risen from the dead."

10 And His disciples asked Him, saying, "Why then do the scribes say E-li'-jah must come first?

11 Jesus answered and said to them, "Indeed, E-li'-jah is coming first and will restore all things.

12 "But I say to you that E-li'-jah has come already, and they did not know him but did to him whatever they wished. Likewise the Son of Man is also about to suffer at their hands."

13 Then the disciples understood that He spoke to them of John the Baptist.

14 And when they had come to the multitude, a man came to Him, kneeling down to Him and saying,

15 "Lord, have mercy on my son, for he is an epileptic and suffers severely; for he often falls into the fire and often into the water.

16 "So I brought him to Your disciples, but they could not cure him."

17 Then Jesus answered and said, "O faithless and perverse generation, how long shall I be with you? How long shall I bear with you? Bring him here to Me."

18 And Jesus rebuked the demon, and it came out of him; and the child was cured from that very hour.

19 Then the disciples came to Jesus privately and said, "Why could we not cast it out?"

20 So Jesus said to them, "Because of your unbelief; for assuredly, I say to you, if you have faith as a mustard seed, you will say to this mountain, 'Move from here to there,' and it will move; and nothing will be impossible for you.

21 "However, this kind does not go out except by prayer and fasting."

22 Now while they were staying in Galilee, Jesus said to them, "The Son of Man is about to be betrayed into the hands of men,

23 "and they will kill Him, and the third day He will be raised up. "And they were exceedingly sorrowful.

24 When they had come to Ca-per'na-um, those who received the temple tax came to Peter and said, "Does your Teacher not pay the temple tax?"

25 He said, "Yes." And when he had come into the house, Jesus anticipated him, saying, "What do you think, Simon? From whom do the kings of the earth take customs or taxes, from their sons or from strangers?"

26 Peter said to Him, "From strangers." Jesus said to him, "Then the sons are free.

One can offer prayer without necessarily following through for outcome. Praying is communicating with God in supplication, petition or thanksgiving. A prayer can advance into intercession without one being an intercessor. Intercession requires a certain level of long term dedication and commitment that is not comfortable for the *pray-er*.

Ezekiel 22:30
And I sought for a man among them, that should make up the hedge, and stand in the gap before me for the land, that I should not destroy it: but I found none.

Intercession requires one to stand in the gap for someone or something until a change is seen or the burden is lifted or until the one being prayed for (if individual) is strengthened to the point of taking the prayer **baton**. The work of intercession is not a human undertaking; rather it is a spirit empowerment that takes on risk and sacrifice. It is an ongoing process and leaves no room for time off or ease of responsibility. Intercession is not a work of feeling but one of commitment and determination.

Philippians 3:12

Not as though I had already attained, either were already perfect: but I follow after, if that I may apprehend that for which also I am apprehended of Christ Jesus.

Intercession can be performed individually or collectively with other believers. When a group is in agreement the power of prayer is magnified. This is seen in the following Scriptures:

Acts 12:3-17 (NKJV)

3 And because he saw that it pleased the Jews, he proceeded further to seize Peter also. Now it was during the Days of Unleavened Bread.

4 So when he had apprehended him, he put him in prison, and delivered him to four squads of soldiers to keep him, intending to bring him before the people after Passover.

5 Peter was therefore kept in prison, but constant prayer was offered to God for him by the church.

6 And when Her'od was about to bring him out, that night Peter was sleeping, bound with two chains between two soldiers; and the guards before the door were keeping the prison.

7 Now behold, an angel of the Lord stood by him, and a light shone in the prison; and he struck Peter on the side and raised him up, saying, "Arise quickly!" And his chains fell off his hands.

8 Then the angel said to him, "Gird yourself and tie on your sandals;" and so he did. And he said to him, "Put on your garment and follow me."

9 So he went out and followed him, and did not know that what was done by the angel was real, but thought he was seeing a vision.

10 When they were past the first and the second guard posts, they came to the iron gate that leads to the city, which opened to them of its own accord; and they went out and went down one street, and immediately the angel departed from him.

11 And when Peter had come to himself, he said, "Now I know for certain that the Lord has sent His angel, and has delivered me from the hand of Her'od and from all the expectation of the Jewish people."

12 So, when he had considered this, he came to the house of Mary, the mother of John whose surname was Mark, where many were gathered together praying.

13 And as Peter knocked at the door of the gate, a girl named Rho`da came to answer.

14 When she recognized Peter's voice, because of her gladness she did not open the gate, but ran in and announced that Peter stood before the gate.

15 But they said to her, "You are beside yourself!" Yet she kept insisting that it was so. So they said, "It is his angel."

16 Now Peter continued knocking; and when they opened the door and saw him, they were astonished.

17 But motioning to them with his hand to keep silent, he declared to them how the Lord had brought him out of the prison. And he said, "Go, tell these things to James and to the brethren." And he departed and went to another place.

In addition to the prompting of intercession for situations that are directed by the Spirit of God the Bible admonishes us to pray for those in positions of authority as it states in 1 Timothy 2:1-2, **1** Therefore I exhort first of all that supplications, prayers, intercessions, and giving of thanks be made for all men, **2** for kings and all who are in authority, that we may lead a quiet and peaceable life in all godliness and reverence (NKJV).

A pray-er can be pulled into interceding for something specific because it is of vital importance to the Kingdom of God and the movement in one's life. The pray-er does not have to be an intercessor but is used by the Lord to extend the Hand of God's mercy, petitioning the Lord God Almighty, because the issues at hand can have a devastating effect on the life and quality of life of the person(s). The Lord can use willing people to fulfill His plans for

Kingdom work, thereby advancing the work of the kingdom in the lives of His people that He loves. The Prophet Amos declared:

Amos 7:14-16

14 Then answered Amos, and said to Am-a-zi'ah, I was no prophet, neither was I a prophet's son; but I was an herdman, and a gatherer of sycamore fruit:

15 And the LORD took me as I followed the flock, and the LORD said unto me, Go, prophesy unto my people Israel.

16 Now therefore hear thou the word of the LORD: Thou sayest, Prophesy not against Israel, and drop not thy word against the house of Isaac.

Remember we have an advocate with God. It is Jesus who intercedes for us as believers so as we join corporately with others we bond our prayers with the greatest of intercessors. Romans 8:34 declares, "Who is he who condemns? It is Christ who died, and furthermore is also risen, who is even at the right hand of God, who also makes intercession for us (NKJV).

Prayer: *Father thank you for your wisdom in guiding us your children to take on your attributes and pray your heart. Thank you for the opportunity to show compassion to others as we remember them in prayer in Jesus' name. Amen.*

NOTES

CHAPTER SIX

Developing Focus and Consistency in Prayer

ENDURE

Focus defined means to concentrate, to adjust to a center point, as a camera lens brings its subject into focus to get a clear image. The natural world is a mirror of what happens in the spiritual realm. The believer should apply spiritual principles to make natural applications to reach desired results — answers to prayer. Staying attuned to the specific need rather than the end result will come if you stay the course. Answers to prayer do not always yield immediate results. The word intercession can be looked at as entering into an agreement, then being persistent, hour by hour, day by day, month by month, even year by year in some cases. Always remember that we are instruments in the skillful hands of our Father. The Apostle Paul proclaims in Galatians 6:9, "And let us not lose heart and grow weary and faint in acting nobly and doing right, for in due time and at the appointed season we shall reap, if we do not loosen and relax our courage and faint" (AMP).

A key point to remember in prayer is that God always hears our petitions and requests. Psalm 34:15 says, "The eyes of the LORD are on the righteous, And His ears are open to their cry" (NKJV). Since God is omnipotent and omnipresent He is not limited by the boundaries of mankind or any evil force that would try to come against Him. Sometimes anxiety, fear or confusion makes it difficult to hear the heart of God. Remember there is an evil force, Satan and he is the most deceptive being of all time. He will challenge what is spoken or revealed to you by God. When the challenges come we have to center on the most solid foundation we have – the Bible. Although Satan's challenge comes as no surprise — even Jesus the very Son of God, was pressed by Satan right after Jesus was commissioned to begin his ministerial work on the earth. But Jesus countered the plans of Satan by using the written Word to combat his attack as seen in the Gospel of Luke.

Luke 4:1-13 (NKJV)

1 Then Jesus, being filled with the Holy Spirit, returned from the Jordan and was led by the Spirit into the wilderness,

2   being tempted for forty days by the devil. And in those days He ate nothing, and afterward, when they had ended, He was hungry.

3   And the devil said to Him, "If You are the Son of God, command this stone to become bread."

4   But Jesus answered him, saying, "It is written, 'Man shall not live by bread alone, but by every word of God.'"

5   Then the devil, taking Him up on a high mountain, showed Him all the kingdoms of the world in a moment of time.

6   And the devil said to Him, "All this authority I will give You, and their glory; for this has been delivered to me, and I give it to whomever I wish.

7   "Therefore, if You will worship before me, all will be Yours."

8   And Jesus answered and said to him, "Get behind Me, Satan! For it is written, 'You shall worship the LORD your God, and Him only you shall serve.'"

9   Then he brought Him to Jerusalem, set Him on a pinnacle of the temple, and said to Him, "If You are the Son of God, throw Yourself down from here.

10 "For it is written: He shall give His angels charge over you, To keep you,'

11 "and, 'In their hands they shall bear you up, Lest you dash your foot against a stone.'"

12 And Jesus answered and said to him, "It has been said, 'You shall not tempt the LORD your God.'"

13 Now when the devil had ended every temptation, he departed from Him until an opportune time.

RESULTS ARE NOT ALWAYS IMMEDIATE

Today's society has been shaped to expect instantaneous results. A quick search on a computer's web browser like Google, can show thousands of results in fractions of a second. A cell phone allows a call to be made in seconds almost anywhere in the world. Stop at an ATM (Automated Teller Machine) and you can get money in minutes without ever having to wait in line. Technology is changing all the time. Before the promoters of one product have reached their market, watch out because another is in the making and endless lines of seekers are eager to dive into the next technological advancement.

As change takes place through intercession the key is to continue to be diligent. Focus is required because of all the potential distracters around you. Nehemiah was a Hebrew layman who had been the cupbearer for a foreign king. After interceding for his people, Nehemiah was sanctioned by God to take on the **monumental** task of rebuilding the walls of Jerusalem. Opposition and discouragement rose up quickly in the form of three **antagonists** who sought to instill fear and stop the repair. But despite their best efforts to build a **coalition** against Nehemiah he would not be moved as seen in the Book of Nehemiah.

Nehemiah 2:19 (NKJV)

But when San-bal'lat the Hor'o-nite, To-bi'ah the Am'mon-ite official, and Ge'shem the Arab heard of it, they laughed us to scorn and despised us, and said, "What is this thing that you are doing? Will you rebel against the king?"

Nehemiah 4:1-23 (NKJV)

1 But it so happened, when San-bal'lat heard that we were rebuilding the wall, that he was furious and very indignant, and mocked the Jews.

2 And he spoke before his brethren and the army of Samaria, and said, "What are these feeble Jews doing? Will they fortify themselves? Will they offer sacrifices? Will they complete it in a day? Will they revive the stones from the heaps of rubbish — stones that are burned?"

3 Now To-bi'ah the Am'mon-ite was beside him, and he said, "Whatever they build, if even a fox goes up on it, he will break down their stone wall."

4 Hear, O our God, for we are despised; turn their reproach on their own heads, and give them as plunder to a land of captivity!

5 Do not cover their iniquity, and do not let their sin be blotted out from before You; for they have provoked You to anger before the builders.

6   So we built the wall, and the entire wall was joined together up to half its height, for the people had a mind to work.

7   Now it happened, when San-bal'lat, To-bi'ah, the Arabs, the Am'monites, and the Ash'dod-ites heard that the walls of Jerusalem were being restored and the gaps were beginning to be closed, that they became very angry,

8   and all of them conspired together to come and attack Jerusalem and create confusion.

9   Nevertheless we made our prayer to our God, and because of them we set a watch against them day and night.

10 Then Judah said, "The strength of the laborers is falling, and there is so much rubbish that we are not able to build the wall."

11 And our adversaries said, "They will neither know nor see anything, till we come into their midst and kill them and cause the work to cease."

12 So it was, when the Jews who dwelt near them came, that they told us ten times, "From whatever place you turn, they will be upon us."

13 Therefore I positioned men behind the lower parts of the wall, at the openings; and I set the people according to their families, with their swords, their spears, and their bows.

14 And I looked, and arose and said to the nobles, to the leaders, and to the rest of the people, "Do not be afraid of them. Remember the Lord, great and awesome, and fight for your brethren, your sons, your daughters, your wives, and your houses."

15 And it happened, when our enemies heard that it was known to us, and that God had brought their counsel to nothing, that all of us returned to the wall, everyone to his work.

16 So it was, from that time on, that half of my servants worked at construction, while the other half held the spears, the shields, the bows, and wore armor; and the leaders were behind all the house of Judah.

17 Those who built on the wall, and those who carried burdens, loaded themselves so that with one hand they worked at construction, and with the other held a weapon.

18 Every one of the builders had his sword girded at his side as he built. And the one who sounded the trumpet was beside me.

19 Then I said to the nobles, the rulers, and the rest of the people, "The work is great and extensive, and we are separated far from one another on the wall.

20 "Therefore, wherever you hear the sound of the trumpet, rally to us there, Our God will fight for us."

21 So we labored in the work, and half of the men held the spears from daybreak until the stars appeared.

22 At the same time I also said to the people, "Let each man and his servant stay at night in Jerusalem, that they may be our guard by night and a working party by day."

23 So neither I, my brethren, my servants, nor the men of the guard who followed me took off our clothes, except that everyone took them off for washing.

Nehemiah 5:1-19 (NKJV)

1 And there was a great outcry of the people and their wives against their Jewish brethren.

2 For there were those who said, "We, our sons, and our daughters are many; therefore let us get grain, that we may eat and live."

3 There were also some who said, "We have mortgaged our lands and vineyards and houses, that we might buy grain because of the famine."

4 There were also those who said, "We have borrowed money for the king's tax on our lands and vineyards.

5 "Yet now our flesh is as the flesh of our brethren, our children as their children; and indeed we are forcing our sons and our daughters to be

slaves, and some of our daughters are brought into slavery already. It is not in our power to redeem them, for other men have our lands and vineyards."

6   And I became very angry when I heard their outcry and these words.

7   After serious thought, I rebuked the nobles and rulers, and said to them, "Each of you is exacting usury from his brother." So I called a great assembly against them.

8   And I said to them, "According to our ability we have redeemed our Jewish brethren who were sold to the nations. Now indeed, will you even sell your brethren? Or should they be sold to us?" Then they were silenced and found nothing to say.

9   Then I said, "What you are doing is not good. Should you not walk in the fear of our God because of the reproach of the nations, our enemies?

10 "I also, with my brethren and my servants, am lending them money and grain. Please, let us stop this usury!

11 "Restore now to them, even this day, their lands, their vineyards, their olive groves, and their houses, also the hundredth part of the money and the grain, the new wine and the oil, that you have charged them."

12 So they said, "We will restore it, and will require nothing from them; we will do as you say." Then I called the priests, and required an oath from them that they would do according to this promise.

13 Then I shook out the fold of my garment and said, "So may God shake out each man from his house, and from his property, who does not perform this promise. Even thus may he be shaken out and emptied." And all the assembly said, "Amen!" and praised the LORD. Then the people did according to this promise.

14 Moreover, from the time that I was appointed to be their governor in the land of Judah, from the twentieth year until the thirty-second year of King Ar-ta-xerx'es, twelve years, neither I nor my brothers ate the governor's provisions.

15 But the former governors who were before me laid burdens on the people, and took from them bread and wine, besides forty shekels of silver; Yes, even their servants bore rule over the people, but I did not do so, because of the fear of God.

16 Indeed, I also continued the work on this wall, and we did not buy any land. All my servants were gathered there for the work.

17 Moreover there were at my table were one hundred and fifty Jews and rulers, besides those who came to us from the nations around us.

18 Now that which was prepared daily was one ox and six choice sheep; also fowl were prepared for me, and once every ten days an abundance of all kinds of wine; yet in spite of this I did not demand the governor's provisions, because the bondage was heavy on this people.

19 Remember me, my God, for good, according to all that I have done for this people.

Nehemiah 6:1-19 (NKJV)

1 Now it happened when San-bal'lat, To-bi'ah, Ge'shem the Arab, and the rest of our enemies heard that I had rebuilt the wall, and that there were no breaks left in it (though at that time I had not hung the doors in the gates),

2 that San-bal'lat and Ge'shem sent to me, saying, "Come, let us meet together among the villages in the plain of O'no. But they thought to do me harm.

3 So I sent messengers to them, saying, "I am doing a great work, so that I cannot come down. Why should the work cease while I leave it and go down to you?"

4 But they sent me this message four times, and I answered them in the same manner.

5 Then San-bal'lat sent his servant to me as before, the fifth time, with an open letter in his hand.

6 In it was written: It is reported among the nations, and Ge'shem says,

that you and the Jews plan to rebel; therefore, according to these rumors, you are rebuilding the wall, that you may be their king.

7   And you have also appointed prophets to proclaim concerning you at Jerusalem, saying, "There is a king in Judah!" Now these matters will be reported to the king. So come, therefore, and let us consult together.

8   Then I sent to him, saying, "No such things as you say are being done, but you invent them in your own heart."

9   For they all were trying to make us afraid, saying, "Their hands will be weakened in the work, and it will not be done." Now therefore, O God, strengthen my hands.

10 Afterward I came to the house of She-mai'ah the son of De-lai'ah, the son of Me-het'a-bel, who was a secret informer; and he said, "Let us meet together in the house of God, within the temple, and let us close the doors of the temple, for they are coming to kill you; indeed, at night they will come to kill you."

11 And I said, "Should such a man as I flee? And who is there such as I who would go into the temple to save his life? I will not go in!"

12 Then I perceived that God had not sent him at all, but that he pronounced this prophecy against me because To-bi'ah and San-bal'lat had hired him.

13 For this reason he was hired, that I should be afraid and act that way and sin, so that the might have occasion for an evil report, that they might reproach me.

14 My God, remember To'bi'ah and San'bal'at, according to these their works, and the prophetess No-a-di'ah and the rest of the prophets who would have made me afraid.

15 So the wall was finished on the twenty-fifth day of E'lul, in fifty-two days.

16 And it happened, when all our enemies heard of it, and all the nations around us saw these things, that they were very disheartened in their own eyes; for they perceived that this work was done by our God.

17 Also in those days the nobles of Judah sent many letters to To-bi'ah, and the letters of To-bi'ah came to them.

18 For many in Judah were pledged to him, because he was the son-in-law of Shech-a-ni'ah the son of A'rah, and his son Je-ho-ha'nan had married the daughter of Me-shul'lam the son of Ber-e-chi'ah.

19 Also they reported his good deeds before me, and reported my words to him. To-bi'ah sent letters to frighten me.

Like the wall builder fixed on his task those called to prayer and intercession must maintain a singular **perspective** to accomplish what they are called to do.

Prayer: *Dear Heavenly Father, thank you for teaching us your precepts and for your strengthening and empowering us to stay fixed and focused on the assignment you have called and commissioned us to do. As Paul said, those you called you have also equipped (Ephesians 6:10; Hebrews 13:21) in Jesus' name. Amen.*

NOTES

CHAPTER SEVEN

<u>Discerning the Longevity of the Prayer Group</u>

SHORT TERM PRAYER TO GET A SEASONAL ANSWER

Determining the life cycle of a prayer group is a critical question to which the group must obtain an answer. The key point centers on understanding the mission of the group and the **juncture** at which it has accomplished its assignment. Sometimes the corporate gathering effort may be formed to spotlight a specific event. Sometimes a corporate gathering may be formed to pray for a short-term need. In the early church the Sanhedrin, the high council of the Jews, challenged the apostles to stop preaching about Jesus. Against the possibility of physical abuse the apostles not only continued to proclaim the works of the Messiah but prayed for even greater boldness to do so:

Acts 4:23-31

23 And being let go, they went to their own company, and reported all that the chief priests and elders had said unto them.

24 And when they heard that, they lifted up their voice to God with one accord, and said, Lord, thou art God, which hast made heaven, and earth, and the sea, and all that in them is:

25 Who by the mouth of thy servant David hast said, why did the heathen rage, and the people imagined vain things?

26 The kings of the earth stood up, and the rulers were gathered together against the Lord, and against his Christ.

27 For of a truth against thy holy child Jesus, whom thou hast anointed, both Herod, and Pontius Pilate, with the Gentiles, and the people of Israel, were gathered together,

28 For to do whatsoever thy hand and thy counsel determined before to be done.

29 And now, Lord, behold their threatenings: and grant unto thy servants, that with all boldness they may speak thy word,

30 By stretching forth thine hand to heal; and that signs and wonders may be done by the name of thy holy child Jesus.

31 And when they had prayed, the place was shaken where they were assembled together; and they were all filled with the Holy Ghost, and they spake the word of God with boldness.

CONTINUAL LONG-TERM PRAYER

In some cases the group may be called to extended or ongoing prayer. Some groups in the Middle East have continuous prayer every hour of the day for the church and the drawing in of those who don't yet know the Messiah. Always know that if the group needs clarity and guidance it can always turn to the Lord for wisdom in the matter. James 1:5 says, "If any of you lack wisdom, let him ask of God, that giveth to all men liberally, and upbraideth not; and it shall be given him." Length of time may also depend on the situation or what God has spoken into your heart. One should be sensitive to the heart of God, as not to put all prayer needs in the same pool. Each prayer request should be viewed separately and the intensity based on the situation.

Some circumstances demand long-term prayers and intercession because there are levels of blockages that must be torn down in the spirit in order to get to the root cause of a prayer need to produce **manifestation**. Daniel understood the authority and power of standing as he set himself to a committed endeavor noted Scripturally below:

Daniel 9:3-23

3 And I set my face unto the Lord God, to seek by prayer and supplications, with fasting, and sackcloth, and ashes:

4 And I prayed unto the LORD my God, and made my confession, and said, O Lord, the great and dreadful God, keeping the covenant and mercy to them that love him, and to them that keep his commandments;

5 We have sinned, and have committed iniquity, and have done wickedly, and have rebelled, even by departing from thy precepts and from thy judgments:

6   Neither have we hearkened unto thy servants the prophets, which spake in thy name to our kings, our princes, and our fathers, and to all the people of the land.

7   O Lord, righteousness belongeth unto thee, but unto us confusion of faces, as at this day; to the men of Judah, and to the inhabitants of Jerusalem, and unto all Israel, that are near, and that are far off, through all the countries whither thou hast driven them, because of their trespass that they have trespassed against thee.

8   O Lord, to us belongeth confusion of face, to our kings, to our princes, and to our fathers, because we have sinned against thee.

9   To the Lord our God belong mercies and forgivenesses, though we have rebelled against him;

10 Neither have we obeyed the voice of the LORD our God, to walk in his laws, which he set before us by his servants the prophets.

11 Yea, all Israel have transgressed thy law, even by departing, that they might not obey thy voice; therefore the curse is poured upon us, and the oath that is written in the law of Moses the servant of God, because we have sinned against him.

12 And he hath confirmed his words, which he spake against us, and against our judges that judged us, by bringing upon us a great evil: for under the whole heaven hath not been done as hath been done upon Jerusalem.

13 As it is written in the law of Moses, all this evil is come upon us: yet made we not our prayer before the LORD our God, that we might turn from our iniquities, and understand thy truth.

14 Therefore hath the LORD watched upon the evil, and brought it upon us: for the LORD watched upon the evil, and brought it upon us: for the LORD our God is righteous in all his works which he doeth: for we obeyed not his voice.

15 And now, O Lord our God, that hast brought thy people forth out of the land of Egypt with a mighty hand, and hast gotten thee renown, as at

this day; we have sinned, we have done wickedly.

16 O Lord, according to all thy righteousness, I beseech thee, let thine anger and thy fury be turned away from thy city Jerusalem, thy holy mountain: because for our sins, and for the iniquities of our fathers, Jerusalem and thy people are become a reproach to all that are about us.

17 Now therefore, O our God, hear the prayer of thy servant, and his supplications, and cause thy face to shine upon thy sanctuary that is desolate, for the Lord's sake.

18 O my God, incline thine ear, and hear; open thine eyes, and behold our desolations, and the city which is called by thy name: for we do not present our supplications before thee for our righteousnesses, but for thy great mercies.

19 O Lord, hear; O Lord, forgive; O Lord, hearken and do; defer not, for thine own sake, O my God: for thy city and thy people are called by thy name.

20 And whiles I was speaking, and praying, and confessing my sin and the sin of my people Israel, and presenting my supplication before the LORD my God for the holy mountain of my God;

21 Yea, whiles I was speaking in prayer, even the man Ga'bri-el, whom I had seen in the vision at the beginning, being caused to fly swiftly, touched me about the time of the evening oblation.

22 And he informed me, and talked with me, and said, O Daniel, I am now come forth to give thee skill and understanding.

23 At the beginning of thy supplications the commandment came forth, and I am come to shew thee; for thou art greatly beloved: therefore understand the matter, and consider the vision.

Staying focused is pivotal in having conversations with God throughout each and every day that we live and breathe. You must have a conversation with God from the very beginning of life — school, job, travel, marriage, etc. In Willie's words, we often over steer by making promises that God never asked us to make. Some examples of over steering are: Lord if you get me 'out of this,' what ever your 'this' is, God if you bless me with a job, 'I will…,' Father if you manifest healing in my body, 'I will serve you all my days,' etc, or whatever promise that you make at that time. God is love and He does not love us any less when we do wrong. As a matter of fact "there isn't anything we can do to earn His love or to stop Him from loving us for that matter."[10] The Scripture assures us of God's great love in the following verses:

1 John 4:8-10

8   He that loveth not knoweth not God; for God is love.

9   In this was manifested the love of God toward us, because that God sent his only begotten Son into the world, that we might live through him.

10 Herein is love, not that we loved God, but that he loved us, and sent his Son to be the propitiation (satisfy God's anger TLB) for our sins.

In a recent sermon discourse, Willie created the perfect setting in illustrating various scenarios that Jesus engaged in while interacting with different ones as He taught. Several subject matters were, "Get Ready," which entailed three things: (1) Conversation. Jesus surrounded Himself with people of variety outside of a building. (2) Time. This transcends the period from planting of seed to harvest." and (3) Wait. Being still to listen for the sound of the Spirit word as it bursts inside of our spirit womb. The gentle rush we receive from the Holy Spirit gives us instructions and guidance for our spiritual growth.

Our conversation with the Lord helps to keep our thoughts focused on Heavenly things. Then we see others as the Kingdom sees them with compassion and love. Having patience to wait for God's inward word to us will ultimately bring forth fruit. When we allow the Word to grow in us, many things that are not good for our spiritual walk are broken in our lives. This time with the Lord will expose bad habits and deter us from entering into unhealthy conversations with others. As a result, we gain much needed direction.

These talks provide insight to see and experience God's Kingdom power and the benefit of kingdom work. Also, if we are willing to allow His Word to take root then waiting can become a joy with great expectations, knowing that the Lord always produces the best in us for His glory. Our waiting with joy shapes our mind to the mind of Christ. If we are willing to freely give ourselves to Him to allow the Lord to do what is necessary even when it may not feel good, our willingness to endure can empower us to see the Lord's Kingdom come in our lives. What a joy it is to fellowship with the Lord. As the five wise virgins received great joy and peace with Jesus, so can we have peace in our conversations with the Lord God, Jesus Christ and the Holy Spirit.

Conversations with God require that time is spent listening; His promises are sure. "Time is a hard taskmaster. Time is a created thing to keep order in the earth. You were never meant to serve time — it was meant to serve mankind."[11]

The Gospel according to Matthew is the platform from which Willie built his message.

Matthew 25: 1-13

1 THEN shall the kingdom of heaven be likened unto ten virgins, which took their lamps, and went forth to meet the bridegroom.

2 And five of them were wise, and five were foolish.

3 They that were foolish took their lamps, and took no oil with them:

4 But the wise took oil in their vessels with their lamps.

5 While the bridegroom tarried, they all slumbered and slept.

6 And at midnight there was a cry made, Behold, the bridegroom cometh; go ye out to meet him.

7 Then all those virgins arose, and trimmed their lamps.

8 And the foolish said unto the wise, Give us of your oil; for our lamps are gone out.

9 But the wise answered, saying, Not so; lest there be not enough for us and you: but go ye rather to them that sell, and buy for yourselves.

10 And while they went to buy, the bridegroom came; and they that were ready went in with him to the marriage: and the door was shut.

11 Afterward came also the other virgins, saying, Lord, Lord, open to us.

12 But he answered and said, Verily I say unto you, I know you not.

13 Watch therefore, for ye know neither the day nor the hour wherein the Son of man cometh.

The beginning stage of the ten virgins was the same. They all seem to have all things equal; it would seem that the conversation of the five virgins shifted to some other thoughts that caused them to lose focus of why they had been set aside and for whom they had been set aside. We must exercise care to make sure that our conversation is one that pleases our Lord at all times. Our time should be used wisely so that the Lord is pleased with what we do daily. There are some circumstances where waiting would require an effort and some persistence. The instructions were for the virgins to arrive at a place and wait to be received. Waiting is a required duty of the believers to grow and expand in one's life and lifestyle for Kingdom purpose. God says, 'slow down,' but we keep going — burning oil in our lamps.

Prayer: Thank you Lord for teaching us to understand the timing and extent to which we petition for the work that needs to be accomplished both on Earth and in Heaven. As we call upon you let our ears open to hear the answer that you are sure to provide. When patience is required we rest in you and trust you as we tarry in faith in Jesus' name. Amen.

NOTES

I'AM SUPPOSE TO CALL SALLY.
MAN I GOTTA DO OVERTIME AT WORK.
ESPN

CHAPTER EIGHT

<u>Handling Distractions</u>

HOW DOES ONE HANDLE THE DISTRACTIONS THAT COME?
During an episode of the movie "Star Wars," the group seeking to fight against evil was preparing to destroy the enemy's most lethal instrument called the Death Star. Against all odds the heroes launched an attack against the giant weapon nearly the size of a small moon. As they sped onto the surface of the Death Star small enemy ships followed in hot pursuit. One man surrounded by a host of escorts was chosen to hit the energy source that would cause annihilation of the enemy's super ship. Despite destruction and chaos around him while ships were blowing up one by one, the hero stayed locked onto a display screen in frontal view. Along with the graphics shown a message was conveyed to him. It was simply this — stay on target, stay on target!

As believers we must stay on target. But how do we accomplish our mission with all the distractions going on around us?

Be assured that distractions will come. They may come from you, from other people, other things, or from the enemy. Sometimes things that are important and need your immediate attention can pull you away. Other times things only appear to be important. Then there are times when your mind may just drift along leading you to become distracted by things that are not important at all. It's essential to prioritize and prayerfully decide what needs to be done now and what can wait till later.

Restraint is crucial to weeding out distractions that occur over time based on one's level of determination and diligence. Paul admonished the Corinthian church by stating, "Therefore, my beloved brethren, be ye stedfast, unmoveable, always abounding in the work of the Lord, forasmuch as ye know that your labour is not in vain in the Lord" (I Corinthians 15:58).

Once the distraction has been dealt with it is time to change your priorities. Sometimes, in order to do this, you have to stop and spend time in His presence worshipping, praising, and praying. Other times just sit quietly, resting, while listening for God to speak. As David said: "Rest in the LORD, and wait patiently for him: fret not thyself because of him who prospereth in his way, because of the man who bringeth wicked devices to pass." (Psalm 37:7).

There are also times when the Truth of the Lord has to be declared over the distractions by opening your mouth and saying what the Lord has said in His Word about the situation. The following confessions based in Scripture and the Scripture references declare:

1 Corinthians 2:16b NKJV
I have the mind of Christ so I can do what needs to be done. I can focus and stay tuned in to the Holy Spirit.

Isaiah 50:7
I will set my face like flint looking neither to the left nor to the right but continue on until my task is complete.

Proverbs 4:25-27 AMP
25 Let your eyes look right on [with fixed purpose], and let your gaze be straight before you.

26 Consider well the path of your feet, and let all your ways be established and ordered aright.

27 Turn not aside to the right hand or to the left; remove your foot from evil.

Philippians 4:13 NKJV
I can do all things through Christ which strengthens me.

Psalm 37:23a NKJV
My steps are ordered by the Lord.

Psalm 32:8 AMP
He protects and directs me.

***Prayer:** Lord teach us to stay on target. We thank you that when we have sweeping thoughts that draw us away from the call to pray that we purpose in our hearts not to be distracted by the works of the enemy. We walk in perfect peace when our minds are stayed on you and the work you have called us to in Jesus' name. Amen.*

NOTES

RIDDLE

The Parable of the Eagles and the Vine   - Ezekiel 17:2-10

2 Son of man, put forth a riddle, and speak a parable unto the house of Israel; 3 And say, Thus saith the Lord GOD; A great eagle with great wings, longwinged, full of feathers, which had divers colours, came unto Lebanon, and took the highest branch of the cedar: 4 He cropped off the top of his young twigs, and carried it into a land of traffic; he set it in a city of merchants. 5 He took also of the seed of the land, and planted it in a fruitful field; he placed it by great waters, and set it as a willow tree. 6 And it grew, and became a spreading vine of low stature, whose branches turned toward him, and the roots thereof were under him; so it became a vine, and brought forth branches, and shot forth sprigs.

7 There was also another great eagle with great wings and many feathers: and, behold, this vine did bend her roots toward him, and shot forth her branches toward him, that he might water it by the furrows of her plantation. 8 It was planted in a good soil by great waters, that it might bring forth branches, and that it might bear fruit, that it might be a goodly vine.

9 Say thou, Thus saith the Lord GOD; Shall it prosper? Shall he not pull up the roots thereof, and cut off the fruit thereof, that it wither? it shall wither in all the leaves of her spring, even without great power or many people to pluck it up by the roots thereof. 10 Yea, behold, being planted, shall it prosper? shall it not utterly wither, when the east wind toucheth it? it shall wither in the furrows where it grew.

CHAPTER NINE

Trials and Tribulations

WHAT DOES ONE DO WHEN TRIALS AND TRIBULATIONS COME UPON THE UNIT?

Increase your tenacity to stand and pray through until the burden is lifted knowing that you have the authority of the Word that will sustain you to victory. "And we desire that every one of you do shew the same diligence to the full assurance of hope unto the end:" (Hebrews 6:11). Jesus said, "… In the world you have tribulation and trials and distress and frustration; but be of good cheer [take courage; be confident, certain, undaunted]! For I have overcome the world. [I have deprived it of power to harm you and have conquered it for you] (John 16:33b AMP).

So, when trials and tribulations come, when at times it seems like the Lord is nowhere to be found, press in and press on. Press into the Word of God. Press into prayer, praise, and worship. Press on knowing that your Deliverer is with you and that He cannot lie. He tells us in Hebrews 13:5b, "I will never fail you or abandon you" (CJB). "God is not a human who lies or a mortal who changes his mind. When he says something, he will do it; when he makes a promise, he will fulfill it" (Numbers 23:19 CJB). "For I am the LORD, I do not change; (Malachi 3:6a NKJV).

Sometimes our first reaction, when trials and tribulations come, is to ease back on or completely quit what the Lord told us to do. Kick it up a notch or two instead. Increase your praying, praising, worshipping, reading and meditating on the Word and time alone with the Lord. This puts pressure on the enemy and strengthens you. The very Presence of the Lord is in our praise. It is said in Psalm 22:3-5, 3 "But you are holy, Who inhabit the praises of Israel. 4 Our fathers trusted in You; They trusted, and You delivered them. 5 They cried to You, and were delivered; They trusted in You and were not ashamed" NKJV). This pattern also creates a greater ability for you and/or the group to hear more clearly any specifics the Spirit may be giving you about this season of trials, such as: are you still following the plan God set for you, are there areas that need correction, and how to deal with what is happening? "Call to Me and I will answer you and show you great and mighty things, fenced in and hidden, which you do not know (do not distinguish and recognize, have knowledge of and understand)" (Jeremiah 33:3 AMP). Do as Joshua was commanded by the Lord to do. "This Book of the Law shall not depart from your mouth, but you shall meditate in it day and night, that you may observe to do according to all that is written in it. For then you will make your way prosperous, and then you will have good success" (Joshua 1:8 NKJV).

We may not go to a mountaintop or a desert place as Jesus did; still He has modeled for us the need to have time alone with God as shown in these Scripture references:

Matthew 14:23 NKJV
And when He had sent the multitudes away, He went up on a mountain by Himself to pray. And when evening had come, He was alone there.

Luke 5:16 NKJV
So He Himself often withdrew into the wilderness and prayed.

Mark 1:35 AMP
And in the morning, long before daylight, He got up and went out to a deserted place, and there He prayed.

Luke 6:12
And it came to pass in those days, that he went out into a mountain to pray, and continued all night in prayer to God.

Psalm 119:15-16 NKJV
15 I will meditate on Your precepts, And contemplate Your ways.

16 I will delight myself in Your statues; I will not forget Your word.

1 Peter 3:12 NKJV
"For the eyes of the LORD are on the righteous, And His ears are open to their prayers; But the face of the LORD is against those who do evil."

Psalm 96:9a NKJV
Oh, worship the Lord in the beauty of holiness!

Hebrews 13:15 AMP

Through Him, therefore, let us constantly and at all times offer up to God a sacrifice of praise, which is the fruit of lips that thankfully acknowledge and confess and glorify His name.

Romans 12:12 EXB

Be joyful because you have hope [Rejoice in hope]. Be patient [Endure] when trouble comes [in suffering/tribulations], and pray at all times [faithfully; with persistence/perseverance].

Paul says in 2 Timothy 1:13-14 TLB

13 Hold tightly to the pattern of truth I taught you, especially concerning the faith and love Christ Jesus offers you.

14 Guard well the splendid, God-given ability you received as a gift from the Holy Spirit who lives within you.

And don't forget to pray for and encourage one another. Galatians 6:2 TLB, tells us "Share each other's troubles and problems, and so obey our Lord's command." And 1 Thessalonians 5:11 TLB says, "So encourage each other to build each other up, just as you are already doing."

Maintain a positive approach as trials spur you to growth as Romans 12:12 declares, "Rejoicing in hope; patient in tribulation; continuing instant in prayer;" Temptations test the strength of our endurance. James 1:12 says, "Blessed is the man that endureth temptation: for when he is tried, he shall receive the crown of life, which the Lord hath promised to them that love him."

RICK'S RECOLLECTION

In the fall of 1990 I was a young military officer stationed in Germany. Near the end of our field training exercise our division was notified that we were scheduled to deploy to Saudi Arabia in support of Operation Desert Shield. We returned to our home station to prepare all the necessary equipment for shipment to the Middle East. Preparations were made for families left behind and for soldiers deploying to the unknown challenges that lay ahead.

I remember receiving a call from a soldier's mother who exclaimed compassionately, "Bring my son home safe." Suddenly I sensed the weightiness of the request because in my own power I couldn't guarantee that anyone's son would come home safe. So I prayed for their safety. Then in my spirit I heard the Lord say, "You won't lose a single soldier."

Eventually conflict ensued across Kuwait and Iraq. Near the end of the Gulf War I received some shattering news. A message made its way to our battalion headquarters that one of my soldiers had been killed and the next of kin back in the United States had been notified. I was shaken and questioned God. Had I missed what was spoken to me? Had He even made the promise? I went to the Lord in prayer to understand what happened.

Within a short period of time the answer came. I learned that the soldier reported as "dead" had been picked up by the MP (military police)! His armored vehicle had failed during the drive across the Iraqi border. The serviceman who had been declared dead had both the challenge and the pleasure of calling to convince grieving relatives that He was alive indeed!

When the trial came God's act of faithfulness helped strengthen my trust in him. As we gain victories through Christ we gather a reservoir of fulfilled promises. We can draw upon those victories to encourage us for the next battle. David showed an example of this as he prepared to face Goliath:

I Samuel 17:34-36

34 And David said unto Saul, Thy servant kept his father's sheep, and there came a lion, and a bear, and took a lamb out of the flock:

35 And I went after him, and smote him, and delivered it out of his mouth: and when he arose against me, I caught him by his beard, and smote him, and slew him.

36 Thy servant slew both the lion and the bear: and this uncircumcised Philistine shall be as one of them, seeing he hath defied the armies of the living God.

Prayer: *Father you continue to crown us with wisdom and understanding of your Word as we walk this walk daily. Thank you for teaching us how to endure on a daily basis. Help us not to shun the trials that come our way for they refine us in becoming more like you. In Jesus' name we pray. Amen.*

NOTES

CHAPTER TEN

<u>Keys to Remember</u>

ASK THE GOD OF GODS FOR DIRECTION

God's guidance is paramount to the believer in any decision making process. He is the most powerful resource in the universe; yet many times we only think to ask His insights when we have exhausted every other means that comes to mind. His answers may come to us through His word, a declaration given to another believer or by that teaching force, the Holy Spirit, who resides in us. Whatever the mechanism, the answer must always past the **litmus test** of being in agreement with what the Bible says because sometimes what seems like a "revelation" may not match up with what has been revealed in His Word. There are many voices speaking in the world. Not all of them speak truth. Jesus said to His disciples, "For false christs and false prophets will arise and show great signs and wonders. So as to deceive, if possible, even the elect" (Matthew 24:24 NKJV). The Apostle John writes, 1 "BELOVED, do not believe every spirit, but test the spirits, whether they are of God; because many false prophets have gone out into the world" 2 By this you know the Spirit of God: Every spirit that confesses that Jesus Christ has come in the flesh is of God, (1 John 4:1-2 NKJV).

HEARING GOD'S VOICE

Oftentimes, we don't get answers because we don't ask questions. The Scripture admonishes in James 4:2-3 GNT, "You want things, but you cannot have them, so you are ready to kill; you strongly desire things, but you cannot get them, so you quarrel and fight. You do not have what you want because you do not ask God for it." 3 "And when you ask, you do not receive it, because your motives are bad; you ask for things to use for your own pleasures." But the Lord is able and willing to respond to the questions of those that seek Him. Jesus said, "Ask and it will be given to you; seek, and you will find; knock, and it will be opened to you" (Matthew 7:7 NKJV). In fact when we are placed in certain situations God even provides the words to say and when to say them. So don't be surprised when you ask for guidance in a confusing situation and a Bible verse or a stirring insight comes out of your mouth! The Bible is the believer's guidebook for insight into any difficulty we face in our daily walk. The Lord Jesus declared, **11** "And when they bring you unto the synagogues, and unto magistrates, and powers, take ye no thought how or what thing ye shall answer, or what ye shall say:" **12** "For the Holy Ghost shall teach you in the same hour what ye ought to say" (Luke 12:11-12).

Hearing indicates an attunement to a selective range of sounds. Our natural ears perceive sound across a spectrum of tones that miraculously allows us to hear those we know. Hearing the voice of someone who cares for us is more than just a detection of the senses; it is about a relationship. A newborn baby responds to the soothing, trusting tones of a mother's lullaby. A nervous adolescent on the baseball field grows confident when he hears a reassuring chant of encouragement from a proud parent. In essence we learn to be attentive to those we trust because we have confidence they want to speak constructively into our lives. As our King, the Lord only speaks constructively into our lives and has our best interest at heart. First Corinthians 14:33 says, "For God is not the author of confusion, but of peace, as in all the churches of the saints."

Stay open to the voice of God because the believer is not equipped to do what only God can do. **4** "And when he putteth forth his own sheep, he goeth before them, and the sheep follow him: for they know his voice. **5** "And a stranger will they not follow, but will flee from him: for they know not the voice of strangers." (John 10:4, 5). Remain available and adaptable to change and allow God's anointing to flow through you. We are vessels to be used by God according to His divine will. "But ye are a chosen generation, a royal priesthood, an holy nation, a peculiar people; that ye should shew forth the praises of him who hath called you out of darkness into his marvelous light:" (1 Peter 2:9).

Prayer: Lord we thank You that You are the wisest Being that has ever existed and we have a steadfast relationship with You because of the price You paid for our redemption. We look to You as the guiding force that leads us down the path of wisdom and righteousness. We are grateful for the Holy Spirit we can draw upon to point us to truth and understanding in Jesus' name. Amen.

NOTES

CHAPTER ELEVEN

Overcoming the Urge to Quit

There will be a time when it appears that things you have been praying about will not come to pass and you come away feeling discouraged and defeated. Once again, recall to memory God's promises; find out what He has to say in His Word about your situation, and then rehearse the answer to yourself. Declare the truth of the word out loud if necessary. The Lord is waiting to hear His Word and bring it to past. God spoke through His prophet Jeremiah saying, "…I am watching to make sure my words come true" (Jeremiah 1:12b EXB). We have the assurance that "God's Word will not come back to Him empty but do what He sent it to do." The Expanded Bible Version says, "The same thing is true of the words I speak [that go out of my mouth]. They will not return to me empty. They make the things happen that I want to happen [accomplish what I desire/purpose], and they succeed in doing what I send them to do" (Isaiah 55:11 EXB).

Praise and worship, prayer, and the "Word of God, are powerful weapons of spiritual warfare. They are not physical but spiritual and mighty through God for pulling down of strongholds." It is stated this way in the Expanded Bible in II Corinthians 10:4, "We fight with weapons that are different from those the world uses [not merely human weapons; not of the flesh]. Our weapons have power from God that can destroy the enemy's strong places [strongholds; fortresses]…"

In Matthew 7:7-8 AMP Jesus teaches, 7 "Keep on asking and it will be given to you; keep on seeking and you will find; keep on knocking [reverently] and [the door] will be opened to you." 8 "For everyone who keeps on asking receives; and he who keeps on seeking finds; and to him who keeps on knocking, [the door] will be opened."

Our God is not a respecter of persons and what He has done for others He will do for you. Peter states in Acts 10:34 EXB, "…to God every person is the same." "[God does not show favoritism/partiality]" So, keep on asking, and keep on praying till victory comes or the Holy Spirit shows you something else that needs to be done. Follow the command in Galatians 6:9 AMP, "And let us not lose heart and grow weary and faint in acting nobly and doing right, for in due time and at the appointed season we shall reap, if we do not loosen and relax our courage and faint."

If the crushing weight of feelings of failure, defeat, and disappointment lead you to believe the lies of the devil and cause you to fall into doubt and unbelief, remember "the devil is a liar and the father of lies" (John 8:44 NKJV). Therefore, shut out his lies and accusations and get up and "stir up the gift of God that is in you" (II Timothy 1:6 NKJV). Renew your mind and repent, knowing that because "God has such great love for us, He is rich in mercy" (Ephesians 2:4 NKJV). In 1 John 1:9 TLB, the Apostle John tells us, "But if we confess our sins to Him, He can be depended on to forgive us and to cleanse us from every wrong. And it is perfectly proper for God to do this for us because Christ died to wash away our sins."

STAY IN THE FIGHT

Don't stop fighting the good fight of faith I Timothy 6:12 (NKJV), because you have a Helper who will show you the truth and cause you to succeed. (John 16:7,13 AMP) **7** However, I am telling you nothing but the truth when I say it is profitable (good, expedient, advantageous) for you that I go away. Because if I do not go away, the Comforter (Counselor, Helper, Advocate, Intercessor, Strengthener, Standby) will not come to you [into close fellowship with you]; but if I go away, I will send Him to you [to be in close fellowship with you]. **13** But when He, the Spirit of Truth (the Truth-giving Spirit) comes, He will guide you into all the Truth (the whole, full Truth). For He will not speak His own message [on His own authority]; but He will tell whatever He hears [from the Father; He will give the message that has been given to Him], and He will announce and declare to you the things that are to come [that will happen in the future]. What He begins He will finish, Philippians 1:6 (NKJV). Continue to walk by faith and not by sight because "We live [walk] by what we believe [faith], not by what we can see [sight]." II Corinthians 5:7 (EXB). "And having done all the crisis demands then stand firmly in your place!" (Ephesians 6:13b AMP).

Philippians 1:6 NKJV
"What He begins He will finish"

2 Corinthians 5:7 EXB
"We live [walk] by what we believe [faith], not by what we can see [sight]."

Ephesians 6:13 AMP

"And having done all the crisis demands then stand firmly in your place!"

Ephesians 6:10-13 CJB

10 Finally, grow powerful in union with the Lord, in union with His mighty strength!

11 Use all the armor and weaponry that God provides, so that you will be able to stand against the deceptive tactics of the Adversary.

12 For we are not struggling against human beings, but against the rulers, authorities and cosmic powers governing this darkness, against the spiritual forces of evil in the heavenly realm.

13 So take up every piece of war equipment God provides; so that when the evil day comes, you will be able to resist; and when the battle is won, you will still be standing.

Make it a habit of staying in the positive mode. Do not allow your spiritual dial to drift and pick up frequencies that form a barrier to the voice of God. Allow right thinking and speaking the Word of God to become a way of life. Seek the wisdom and guidance of God. "If any of you lack wisdom, let him ask of God that gives to all men liberally…" (James 1:5a). We were created to win. Find scriptures that bear the testimony of the Patriarchs of old for encouragement. Don't be hesitant about asking the covering of other believers or ministries to help you through dry seasons under the direction of the Holy Spirit. "For as the body is one, and hath many members, and all the members of that one body, being many, are one body: so also is Christ" (1 Corinthians 12:12).

Prayer: Father in the name of Jesus thank You for how you love us! Lord our hope is in Your Name. Even in times of weakness our hope is in Your Name. We hope in Your Name because you are who You say You are and you do what You say you will do. Your Word is Truth and light and life and you are not a God that lies. Therefore, when our hearts are overwhelmed and we feel like quitting, we stir ourselves up, because we remember Your Name. We remember Your Word and Your promises. We remember who You are and how much You love us and how You want to bless us. We recall to mind Your blessing and faithfulness of times past and are encouraged and strengthened. Blessed be the name of the Lord God Almighty! In Jesus' name we pray. Amen.

NOTES

CHAPTER TWELVE

<u>Achieving Victory</u>

VICTORY IS NOT OUT OF REACH. PRAISE GOD!
Our entire relationship with the Lord is based on the belief that He exists. We see evidence of His Supernatural touch on the footprint of the universe every day. The rising and setting of the sun, the birds chirping in the trees, the provision of oxygen for our lungs, the innumerable galaxies that continue to be discovered, and the cells that unite to bring forth a child. The harmony of the existence of the **macroscopic** and **microscopic** worlds shatters the notion that all of creation happened by chance and somehow came in **synchronicity**.

As mankind we have the highest privilege of all the living beings and that is the ability to talk and pray directly to God. He has created us in His image and destined us for greatness because He is great as declared in Genesis 1:27 (NKJV), "So God created man in His own image; in the image of God He created him; male and female He created them." By faith we are able to be victorious and as we endeavor to pray for others they can be victorious too.

We are never without a word of comfort and encouragement to forge ahead no matter what the spiritual terrain depict because God wants to help you and bless you. The Psalmist David and Apostle Paul strengthen us with these words throughout the Bible:

Hebrews 11:6 NKJV
But without faith it is impossible to please Him, for he who comes to God must believe that He is, and that He is a rewarder of those who diligently seek Him.

1 John 5:4 NKJV
For whatever is born of God overcomes the World. And this is the victory that has overcome the world — our faith.

Romans 8:37 NKJV
Yet in all these things we are more than conquerors through Him who loved us.

David said in Psalm 37:23-25 TLB

23 The steps of good men are directed by the Lord. He delights in each step they take.

24 If they fall, it isn't fatal, for the Lord holds them with his hand.

25 I have been young and now I am old. And in all my years I have never seen the Lord forsake a man who loves Him; nor have I seen the children of the godly go hungry.

Psalm 115:13 AMP

"He will bless those who reverently and worshipfully fear the Lord, both small and great."

John 14:16-17 NKJV

16 "And I will pray the Father, and He will give you another Helper, that He may abide with you forever —

17 "the Spirit of truth, whom the world cannot receive, because it neither sees Him nor knows Him; but you know Him, for He dwells with you and will be in you.

Romans 8:31 EXB

"If God is for us no one can defeat us."

Romans 8:37 AMP

"Yet amid all these things we are more than conquerors and gain a surpassing victory through Him Who loved us."

TLB Version

"But despite all this, overwhelming victory is ours through Christ who loved us enough to die for us."

Meditate on what the Lord is saying, which is the answer, and not on the problem. The Devil keeps you focusing on the problem. Your life is already wrapped in victory because Jesus has already secured it by His Blood, so remind yourself that you are already victorious! The Apostle Paul in 1 Corinthians 15:57-58 EXB says, **57** "But we thank God! He gives us the victory through our Lord Jesus Christ." **58** "So my dear [beloved] brothers and sisters, stand strong. Do not let anything move you. Always give yourselves fully to [excel in] the work of the Lord, because you know that your work in the Lord is never wasted [not useless/in vain]."

We are victorious – born to win because we have resurrection power living on the inside of us. "Ye are of God, little children, and have overcome them: because greater is he that is in you than he that is in the world" (1 John 4:4).

Prayer: *Father, in the name of Jesus, I know Your Word is truth and light and life. Your Word says that Jesus has already paid the price for our victory on the cross. So even if I don't see victory manifested in my life right now, I will continue to stand firm on Your promises. In those times when all hope seems lost and defeat seems sure, I will remember and say out of my mouth that You are who You say You are and that You do what You say You will do. Therefore, I will persevere, knowing that my victory is not only within reach, but assured in Jesus' name. Amen.*

NOTES

EPILOGUE

On January 24, 2015, Butler Johnson stepped out of Earth's realm into the full presence of the Lord. He was eulogized in his hometown of Selma, Alabama. Over the course of more than 2 years of weekly prayer sessions Butler grew in the wisdom and knowledge of Christ. Along the way he unashamedly shared his faith and put his hands to the service of the Lord. Even in his last days when asked how he was doing Butler simply responded "I'm blessed".

A roofer by trade, this craftsman was respected by peers and recommended by patrons. This caused Butler to be in constant demand by customers.

Despite his accomplishments Butler would freely acknowledge that the most impactful event in his life was the point when he received Jesus as his Redeemer. Traveling down life's path on this side of Heaven the roofer met another skilled laborer. That laborer's profession was carpentry but his calling was Savior and Lord. At Butler's home going his brother Willie delivered a stirring message when he reflected on the moment the "roofer met the Carpenter" and he was never the same again.

That same "Carpenter" offered up himself for mankind more than 2000 years ago paying a debt that ushered in freedom for eternity to those that believe in him. He fulfilled his calling stated in the Gospel of Luke:

Luke 4:18 - 19

18 The spirit of the Lord is upon me because he has anointed me to preach the gospel to the poor; he hath sent me to heal the broken hearted, to preach deliverance to the captives, and recovering of sight to the blind, to set at liberty those that are bruised.

19 To preach the acceptable year of the Lord.

If you don't have a personal relationship with Jesus, today is your acceptable year of the Lord. Talk to Jesus and tell Him that you are in need of a Savior and you give yourself to Him and desire to live under His banner, His authority and His provision for all eternity. Ask to be filled with the presence of His Spirit.

If you prayed that prayer, welcome brother or sister in Christ into the family. Your prayer has just opened the door to the most important but certainly not the last of many conversations with God.

ANSWER TO RIDDLES

1. What is sweeter than honey? And what is stronger than a lion? (Judges 14:18)

2. The grave; and the barren womb; the earth that is not filled with water; and the fire that saith not, It is enough. (Proverbs 30:16)

3. The Parable is Explained - Ezekiel 17:11:21
   11 Moreover the word of the LORD came unto me, saying, 12 Say now to the rebellious house, Know ye not what these things mean? Tell them, Behold, the king of Babylon is come to Jerusalem, and hath taken the king thereof, and the princes thereof, and led them with him to Babylon; 13 And hath taken of the king's seed, and made a covenant with him, and hath taken an oath of him: he hath also taken the mighty of the land: 14 That the kingdom might be base, that it might not lift itself up, but that by keeping of his covenant it might stand. 15 But he rebelled against him in sending his ambassadors into Egypt, that they might give him horses and much people. Shall he prosper? Shall he escape that doeth such things? Or shall he break the covenant, and be delivered?

   16 As I live, saith the Lord GOD, surely in the place where the king dwelleth that made him king, whose oath he despised, and whose covenant he brake, even with him in the midst of Babylon he shall die. 17 Neither shall Phar'-aoh with his mighty army and great company make for him in the war, by casting up mounts, and building forts, to cut off many persons: 18 Seeing he despised the oath by breaking the covenant, when, lo, he had given his hand, and hath done all these things, he shall not escape.

   19 Therefore thus saith the Lord GOD; As I live, surely mine oath that he hath despised, and my covenant that he hath broken, even it will I recompense upon his own head. 20 And I will spread my net upon him, and he shall be taken in my snare, and I will bring him to Babylon, and will plead with him there for his trespass that he hath trespassed against me. 21 And all his fugitives with all his hands shall fall by the sword, and they that remain shall be scattered toward all winds: and ye shall know that I the LORD hath spoken it.

GLOSSARY

Antagonist - adversary, opponent

Baton - a cylindrical tube passed from one person to another demonstrating an exchange of duty

Behind the veil - the curtain that separated the holy and holy of holies in the temple. A sacred place.

Coalition - a temporary union for a common purpose

Concise - expressing much in a few words

Conversely - just the opposite being true

Fervently yearning - diligently desiring

Inadequacy - insufficiency

Integrate - to form, coordinate or blend into a functioning whole

Juncture - a critical time or state of affairs

Legalism - strict, literal, or excessive conformity to the law or to a religious or moral code

Litmus test - a test in which a single factor (as an attitude) is decisive

Macroscopic - visible to the naked eye

Manifestation - display, demonstration

Microscopic - too tiny to be seen without the use of a microscopic

Monumental - very great

Mundane - of or relating to the world

Obligate - to bind legally or morally

Pray-er - one who focuses on the act of praying

Perspective - the aspect in which a subject or its parts are mentally viewed

Restraint - control over one's feelings

Revelation - an enlightening or astonishing disclosure

Ritualistic - being done as a ritual or ceremonial act

Static - noise or interference produced by electrical or atmospheric disturbances

Stimulating - motivating

Spiritual giant - one considered grounded in the faith and having a strong relationship with God

Stretched out - spiritually striving to connect with God. During this time believers may raise hands or lie with their arms outstretched as a physical act of reverence to God.

Synchronicity - the quality or fact of being simultaneous

Watered - given guidance by the word of God to fill the spiritual thirst just as natural water fulfills our bodily thirst.

ENDNOTES

[1] Gloria Copeland, Daily TV Broadcast, kcm.org

[2] Willie Johnson, Minister, Teacher, Businessman

[3] Mark Twain, www.goodreads.com/quotes/52502

[4] Mary Johnson Lee, Registered Nurse, Housewife, Teacher

[5] Kenneth Copeland, Daily TV Broadcast, kcm.org

[6] John Avanzini, Daily TV Broadcast, Principles of Biblical Economics

[7] Gloria Copeland, Daily Broadcast, kcm.org

[8] sharonglasgow.com/.../susanna wesleys Prayer Apron-Powerful Life Story; July 05, 2013; Internet Article

[9] Bill Winston, Daily TV Broadcast, bwm.org

[10] Kenneth Copeland, Daily TV Broadcast, kcm.org

[11] Bill Winston, Daily TV Broadcast, bwm.org

J AN L PRODUCTIONS LLC
PO BOX 5262
EAST ORANGE, NEW JERSEY 07019-5262
janlproductionsllc@gmail.com

www.ingramcontent.com/pod-product-compliance
Lightning Source LLC
Chambersburg PA
CBHW071926290426
44110CB00013B/1494